CREDIT MAGIC WITH AI:

The Smart Path to a Stellar Score

Unlock Your Financial Potential with Cutting-Edge AI Tools

Copyright © 2024 Ernie Braveboy. All rights reserved.

No part of this publication may be reproduced, distributed, or transmitted in any form or by any means, including photocopying, recording, or other electronic or mechanical methods, without the prior written permission of the publisher, except in the case of brief quotations embodied in critical reviews and certain other noncommercial uses permitted by copyright law.

trademarks and brands within this book are for clarifying purposes only and are the owned by the owners themselves, not affiliated with this document.

Table of Contents

Foreword 1

Introduction 3

PART I

01 The Basics of Credit Scores 8

    1.1 What Is a Credit Score? 10

    1.2 Why Is Your Credit Score Important? 12

    1.3 Factors That Influence Your Credit Score 14

02 An Introduction to Artificial Intelligence 18

    2.1 What Is Artificial Intelligence? 20

    2.2 How AI Is Changing Industries 22

    2.3 AI in Personal Finance: A Primer 25

PART II

03 Monitoring Your Credit with AI 32

    3.1 How AI Monitors Credit 34

    3.2 Best AI Tools for Credit Monitoring 37

    3.3 Setting Up Alerts and Notifications 40

04 AI and Debt Management 43

    4.1 AI in Debt Repayment Strategies 45

    4.2 Prioritizing Your Debts with AI 48

    4.3 Success Stories: AI and Debt Reduction 51

05 Budgeting with AI 54
- 5.1 AI Budgeting Tools: An Overview 57
- 5.2 How to Set Up an AI-Driven Budget 59
- 5.3 Tips for Maintaining a Budget with AI....................................62

PART III

06 Repairing Your Credit Score with AI 70
- 6.1 Identifying Report Errors with AI 73
- 6.2 AI Negotiation Tools for Debt Settlement 75
- 6.3 Strategies for Long-Term Credit Health...............................78

07 Building Your Credit with AI 82
- 7.1 Establishing Credit with AI Assistance.................................84
- 7.2 AI Tools for Building a Credit History..................................87
- 7.3 Preventing Credit Score Decline...90

PART IV

08 Case Studies of AI in Credit Improvement........................ 96
- 8.1 Detailed Analysis of Successful Cases 99
- 8.2 Lessons Learned from AI Credit Enhancements...............102

09 The Future of AI in Credit Management......................... 106
- 9.1 Emerging Trends in AI and Finance...................................109
- 9.2 How to Stay Ahead with AI...112
- 9.3 Ethical Considerations in AI Usage 115

Conclusion 119
- Reflecting on the Journey and Looking Forward....................121

Appendices 124
    Glossary of Terms 126
    FAQs on AI and Credit Management 130
    Resources for Further Exploration 133
Index 136

Foreword

By Dr. Sophia Chen, Leading Expert in Artificial Intelligence and Finance

In the rapidly evolving world of finance, artificial intelligence (AI) has emerged as a transformative force, not just reshaping industries but also fundamentally altering how individuals manage their personal finances. When Ernie Braveboy approached me to write the foreword for "Credit Magic with AI," I was immediately intrigued by the opportunity to discuss the impactful role AI can play in personal credit management—a subject that is becoming increasingly relevant in today's digital age.

Over the past few decades, AI has moved from theoretical research and niche applications into mainstream usage, influencing everything from how we shop and consume media to how we make critical financial decisions. Its integration into personal finance, particularly in credit management, represents a significant leap forward in empowering individuals to take control of their financial destinies. This book does an exceptional job of demystifying AI's role in this process, making it accessible and actionable for anyone looking to enhance their credit score.

Ernie's approach to explaining complex technological concepts in simple, relatable terms is particularly commendable. This book is not just about the theoretical possibilities of AI; it is a practical guide filled with real-world applications and tools that can be implemented immediately by readers. From monitoring credit reports to optimizing debt repayment and budgeting, AI tools offer a smarter, more efficient path to financial health.

The potential of AI to analyze vast amounts of data and provide tailored advice is a game-changer for personal credit improvement. As you delve into this book, you will find numerous examples and case studies that illustrate just how powerful these tools can be. However, it's not just about leveraging technology to fix immediate problems. Ernie also encourages a proactive approach to using AI, which can help prevent future financial pitfalls and strengthen your credit over the long term.

As we stand on the brink of what might be considered a golden era for AI in finance, "Credit Magic with AI" serves as both a guide and a companion for those ready to explore the benefits of this technology. Whether you are struggling with credit issues or simply curious about the future of financial management, this book will provide you with insights and strategies that are both innovative and immensely practical.

I commend Ernie for his forward-thinking approach and am confident that readers will find immense value in these pages. May your journey through "Credit Magic with AI" inspire you to harness the full potential of artificial intelligence to achieve your financial goals.

Introduction

Unlock Your Financial Potential with Cutting-Edge AI Tools

Welcome to a journey that will transform the way you think about your credit score and personal finance. In "**Credit Magic with AI: The Smart Path to a Stellar Score,**" we explore how the latest advancements in artificial intelligence are not just revolutionizing industries but are also key to unlocking your financial potential.

For many, a credit score is a gateway to opportunity, affecting the ability to buy a home, secure a loan, or even determine the interest rates you pay. Yet, understanding and improving your credit score can often seem like a daunting task. This book aims to change that perception by demystifying the role of AI in credit management and making it accessible to everyone.

Why AI?

Artificial intelligence is reshaping the landscape of decision-making and problem-solving across various sectors. In finance, AI's ability to process vast amounts of data rapidly and with precision presents unique opportunities for personal credit enhancement. From identifying errors in credit reports to optimizing debt repayment strategies, AI offers tools that were once available only to financial experts.

In these pages, you will discover:

- **AI-driven insights** that can help you understand and improve your credit score.

- **Practical tools** that monitor, manage, and maximize your financial health.
- **Real-world applications** where AI has helped individuals significantly enhance their credit profiles.

How This Book Will Help You

This book is structured to take you step by step through the landscape of AI in credit management. Starting with a foundation in what credit scores are and how they are calculated, we will move into how AI technologies can be applied to monitor, repair, and enhance your credit. You'll learn about the best AI tools currently available, how to use them effectively, and how to interpret the insights they provide.

We'll also look at real-life case studies to see how others have successfully used AI to overcome their credit challenges. These stories will not only inspire but also provide practical examples of strategies that you can apply directly to your situation.

The Path Forward

As you turn these pages, remember that improving your credit score with AI is a journey. While AI provides the tools and insights, your commitment to applying these innovations is crucial. This book is designed to empower you with knowledge and guide you toward making informed financial decisions that enhance your credit and overall financial stability.

Embark on this transformative path with an open mind and a readiness to embrace technology that can lead you to financial freedom and stability. Let's unlock the magic of AI together and pave the way to a stellar credit score and a brighter financial future.

PART I

Foundations of Credit and AI

This first section of the book lays the groundwork by introducing you to the essential concepts of credit scores and artificial intelligence. Understanding these fundamentals is crucial for leveraging AI effectively in your personal credit management. Here's what we'll cover:

Chapter 1: The Basics of Credit Scores

1.1 What Is a Credit Score?

- Definition and significance of a credit score in personal finance.
- The key elements that make up a credit score.

1.2 Why Is Your Credit Score Important?

- The impact of credit scores on financial opportunities and costs.
- Examples of how credit scores affect everyday life, from loan approvals to interest rates.

1.3 Factors That Influence Your Credit Score

- Detailed look at the components of a credit score: payment history, credit utilization, length of credit history, new credit, and types of credit used.
- Common mistakes that can hurt your credit score.

Chapter 2: An Introduction to Artificial Intelligence

2.1 What Is Artificial Intelligence?

- An overview of AI: definitions, history, and its evolution.
- Different types of AI technologies and how they are used across various sectors.

2.2 How AI Is Changing Industries

- Examples of AI transformations in healthcare, automotive, and entertainment industries.
- Insights into how these changes are indicative of potential shifts in the finance sector.

2.3 AI in Personal Finance: A Primer

- Introduction to the use of AI in personal finance, focusing on credit management.
- Overview of AI tools that are currently reshaping how we manage, predict, and improve financial behaviors.

What You'll Gain from This Part

By the end of this part, you'll have a solid understanding of what a credit score is, why it matters, and how AI is starting to influence the financial decisions individuals make every day. You will be equipped with the necessary knowledge to begin exploring how AI tools can be applied to your personal credit management strategy, setting the stage for more advanced discussions on practical AI applications in the subsequent sections of the book.

This foundational knowledge is not just theoretical; it's the first step toward taking control of your financial destiny using the most advanced tools available today.

01
The Basics of Credit Scores

Understanding the fundamentals of credit scores is essential for anyone looking to manage their finances better. This chapter will explore what credit scores are, why they are important, and what factors influence them. By demystifying these concepts, you'll be better equipped to leverage AI tools to enhance your credit.

1.1 What Is a Credit Score?

- **Definition and Purpose**: A credit score is a numerical expression based on a level analysis of a person's credit files, representing the creditworthiness of an individual. It is used by lenders to evaluate the risk of extending credit or loaning money.

- **How It Is Calculated**: While specific formulas may vary by scoring model, most scores are based on the information in your credit report. We'll look at how these scores are typically calculated and the differences between the major credit scoring models, such as FICO and VantageScore.

1.2 Why Is Your Credit Score Important?

- **Financial Implications:** Your credit score affects the ability to obtain loans, the interest rates payable on loans, and can even impact job opportunities in some sectors. Higher scores generally mean lower financial risk for lenders, which translates to better borrowing terms for the borrower.

- **Long-term Impact**: Beyond immediate financial products, your credit score can affect your housing options, insurance premiums, and even relationships. Understanding its importance can help motivate you to manage your credit responsibly.

1.3 Factors That Influence Your Credit Score

- **Payment History (35%)**: This is the most significant component of your credit score. Late payments, bankruptcies, and other credit missteps can significantly lower your score.

- **Credit Utilization (30%)**: How much of your available credit you're using at any given time. Keeping your utilization low demonstrates that you don't rely solely on credit, which positively affects your score.

- **Length of Credit History (15%)**: Longer credit histories tend to have a positive impact on your score as they provide more data on your spending habits and payment history.

- **Types of Credit in Use (10%)**: A mix of different types of credit (e.g., mortgage, car loans, credit cards) can positively impact your score.

- **New Credit (10%)**: Opening several new credit accounts in a short period can be seen as risky by creditors and might temporarily lower your score.

Key Takeaways

By the end of this chapter, you should have a clear understanding of:

- What a credit score is and why it is a critical financial indicator.

- How credit scores are calculated and the factors that influence them.

- The importance of maintaining a good credit score and the potential consequences of a poor score.

1.1 What Is a Credit Score?

A credit score is a numerical representation of a person's creditworthiness, derived from a detailed analysis of their credit report. This score is used by lenders, landlords, insurers, and sometimes employers to assess how risky it might be to extend credit, lease a property, or offer employment to an individual. It's a crucial metric in financial environments, influencing how financial services are offered and priced.

Definition and Purpose

A credit score simplifies the information in your credit report into a single number that indicates your reliability as a borrower. The score is calculated using a formula that evaluates several aspects of your financial history, focusing on factors like payment reliability and credit usage. Higher scores indicate to lenders and other financial institutions that you are a lower risk, which can lead to better interest rates and terms on loans and credit offers.

How It Is Calculated

Credit scores are calculated using data from your credit reports, which include details of your borrowing history, debt levels, payment regularity, and other financial behaviors. This information is grouped into categories, each of which impacts your overall score to varying degrees. The most commonly known credit scoring models are FICO and VantageScore, which both use similar but slightly different criteria to determine your score:

- **Payment History:** This is the record of your payments on loans and credit accounts, including any late payments. It is the single most significant factor, accounting for approximately 35% of your FICO score. Regular, on-time payments positively affect your score, while late payments, defaults, and bankruptcies have a negative effect.

- **Credit Utilization:** This measures how much of your available credit you are using, expressed as a percentage. It is recommended to keep this ratio under 30% to avoid negatively impacting your score. Credit utilization accounts for roughly 30% of your FICO score.

- **Length of Credit History:** The longer your credit history, the better it is for your score, as it provides more data on your financial behaviors. This category contributes about 15% to your FICO score. It includes the age of your oldest account, the age of your newest account, and the average age of all your accounts.

- **Types of Credit in Use:** Having a variety of credit types (e.g., credit cards, mortgage, auto loans) can positively impact your score because it shows you can manage different types of credit responsibly. This factor makes up about 10% of your FICO score.

- **New Credit:** Opening several new credit accounts in a short period can be seen as risky behavior as it might suggest financial pressure, and thus, this can temporarily lower your score. The influence of new credit on your score also constitutes about 10%.

Key Takeaways

Understanding the composition and calculation of your credit score is fundamental to managing your financial health. A good credit score can open doors to favorable financial opportunities, while a poor score can limit your options. Knowing what affects your score allows you to take specific actions to maintain or improve it. As we progress through this book, we'll explore how AI can be utilized to monitor and enhance these aspects of your credit profile effectively.

1.2 Why Is Your Credit Score Important?

Your credit score is more than just a number on a paper—it's a vital indicator of your financial health and has far-reaching implications across various aspects of your life. Understanding the significance of your credit score is crucial for making informed decisions about managing your finances.

Financial Implications

- **Access to Credit**: The most immediate impact of your credit score is on your ability to obtain loans and credit cards. A higher score can make it easier to get approved for credit, whereas a lower score can severely restrict your access to these financial tools.
- **Interest Rates and Terms**: Your credit score directly affects the terms and interest rates you are offered on loans and credit lines. Higher scores typically qualify you for lower interest

rates, which can save you thousands of dollars over the life of a loan.

- **Credit Limits:** Credit scores can influence the credit limit set by lenders for credit products. A better score can result in higher limits, giving you more financial flexibility.

Broader Life Impact

- **Housing Opportunities:** Landlords often check credit scores when evaluating potential tenants. A good score can improve your chances of securing your desired rental and possibly result in lower security deposits.

- **Employment Opportunities:** In some industries, especially those that involve financial responsibilities, employers may review credit scores as part of the hiring process. A good score can help reassure potential employers of your reliability and responsibility.

- **Insurance Premiums:** Many insurance companies use credit scores to set premium rates for auto and homeowners insurance. A higher score can lead to lower premiums, reflecting a lower risk profile.

Long-term Strategic Planning

- **Financial Planning:** Your credit score affects your long-term financial strategies, including planning for large purchases (like homes or cars) and retirement savings. By affecting your interest rates and access to various credit products, your score plays a key role in how you plan and manage your finances over time.

- **Debt Management**: Understanding the importance of your credit score can motivate you to manage existing debts more effectively and avoid taking on high-cost debts that could jeopardize your financial stability.

Key Takeaways

The importance of your credit score extends beyond mere numbers and influences substantial areas of your personal and financial life. It acts as a key to unlocking opportunities and requires careful management to maintain and improve it. As we delve deeper into the book, we'll explore how AI can assist in enhancing your credit score, not just to improve your financial options today but also to secure a healthier financial future.

1.3 Factors That Influence Your Credit Score

Understanding the factors that influence your credit score is crucial for managing and improving it effectively. Each element of your credit report contributes differently to the overall score. Here, we will break down these components and explain how they impact your creditworthiness.

Payment History

- **Importance**: This is the most critical factor, accounting for approximately 35% of your FICO score.
- **Details**: It includes records of your payments on credit cards, mortgages, loans, and other credit accounts. Lenders are

particularly interested in your reliability in making timely payments.

- **Impact**: Late payments, bankruptcies, foreclosures, and collections can significantly decrease your score. Consistently making payments on time, however, will positively influence your score.

Credit Utilization

- **Importance**: Making up about 30% of your FICO score, credit utilization is the second most influential factor.

- **Details**: This ratio measures the amount of credit you are using relative to your total credit limits. For example, if you have a credit card with a $10,000 limit and you owe $2,000, your credit utilization for that card is 20%.

- **Impact**: Lower utilization rates are viewed favorably and suggest that you are not overextending yourself financially. It is generally recommended to keep your overall credit utilization below 30%.

Length of Credit History

- **Importance**: This factor contributes about 15% to your FICO score.

- **Details**: It considers the age of your oldest account, the age of your newest account, and the average age of all your accounts. It also looks at how long specific credit accounts have been established and how long it has been since those accounts were used.

- **Impact**: A longer credit history provides more data for lenders to evaluate and typically benefits the score, indicating that you have substantial experience managing credit.

Types of Credit in Use

- **Importance**: This accounts for 10% of your FICO score.
- **Details**: Having a mix of different types of credit accounts, such as credit cards, retail accounts, installment loans, finance company accounts, and mortgage loans, can be beneficial.
- **Impact**: This diversity shows that you can handle various types of credit, enhancing your creditworthiness. However, it is not crucial to have one of each type; it's more important to manage credit responsibly.

New Credit

- **Importance**: New credit also influences about 10% of your FICO score.
- **Details**: This includes the number of recently opened accounts and the number of recent inquiries into your credit report, such as credit checks from lenders.
- **Impact**: Opening several new credit accounts in a short period can be interpreted as higher risk, especially for individuals without a long credit history. This can temporarily lower your score.

Key Takeaways

By understanding these five factors, you can strategically influence your credit score. Making timely payments, managing your credit utilization wisely, maintaining older accounts, diversifying your credit portfolio, and being cautious about opening new accounts can all help in building or maintaining a good credit score. As we explore how AI can assist in each of these areas, you'll learn not only to react to your current score but also to proactively shape your future credit standing.

02
An Introduction to Artificial Intelligence

Artificial Intelligence (AI) is revolutionizing numerous industries, and personal finance is no exception. This chapter provides a foundational understanding of AI, explaining what it is, how it operates, and its profound impact across various sectors, including financial services. Understanding these concepts is essential for utilizing AI to manage and improve your credit score effectively.

2.1 What Is Artificial Intelligence?

- **Definition:** AI involves the simulation of human intelligence in machines that are programmed to think and learn like humans. It encompasses a range of technologies capable of observing, understanding, acting, and learning from the outcomes of those actions.
- **Types of AI:** Briefly explore different types of AI, such as machine learning (ML), natural language processing (NLP), and robotics, explaining how each type functions and its relevance to daily applications.

2.2 How AI Is Changing Industries

- **Broad Impacts:** Discuss how AI is being used to transform industries such as healthcare, where it assists in diagnosing diseases faster than traditional methods, or in automotive technology, where AI drives the development of autonomous vehicles.

- **Finance Specific:** Focus on AI's role in transforming the financial industry, particularly in terms of automating trading, personalizing financial advice, and enhancing customer service through chatbots and AI-driven interfaces.

2.3 AI in Personal Finance: A Primer

- **Credit Scoring and Management:** Explain how AI is used to enhance credit scoring models by integrating more data points and patterns that traditional methods might overlook. Discuss AI tools that monitor credit reports, suggest optimal credit utilization, and alert users to potential fraudulent activities.

- **Debt Management:** Detail how AI can help in formulating personalized debt repayment plans based on an individual's financial situation, thereby optimizing debt management strategies.

- **Budgeting and Savings:** Introduce AI tools that analyze spending habits to provide tailored budgeting advice and automate savings. Highlight how these tools can help manage expenditures and increase savings rates without significant manual input from the user.

What You'll Gain from This Part

By the end of this chapter, you will have a solid understanding of:

- **The fundamentals of AI and its various types:** Knowing what AI can do helps demystify its operations and makes its applications in finance more comprehensible and accessible.

- **The transformative impact of AI across industries**: With examples from multiple sectors, you'll be able to appreciate the versatility of AI and its potential beyond just financial applications.

- **Specific applications of AI in personal finance**: You'll see how AI's capabilities can be directly applied to improve your financial health, particularly through better credit management, more efficient debt handling, and smarter budgeting.

This foundation will prepare you to explore the specific AI tools and strategies that can be applied to credit management in the subsequent parts of the book, enhancing both your understanding and your ability to practically apply these technologies to improve your financial standing.

2.1 What Is Artificial Intelligence?

Artificial Intelligence (AI) represents one of the most transformative technological advancements of our time. This section aims to demystify AI, offering a clear understanding of what it is, its various forms, and how it operates. Understanding AI is crucial for harnessing its potential in personal finance and beyond.

Definition of AI

- **Concept Overview**: AI involves machines designed to mimic human intelligence. This includes learning from experiences, understanding complex content, responding to changes in the environment, and making decisions that maximize the chances of successfully achieving a goal.

- **Core Functions**: The fundamental capabilities of AI include learning (the ability to improve performance without explicit programming), reasoning (using the learned information to handle specific tasks), and self-correction (adjusting actions based on new data).

Types of Artificial Intelligence

- **Narrow AI**: Also known as Weak AI, this type of AI is designed to perform a narrow task (e.g., facial recognition or internet searches). Most AI in use today is Narrow AI, which operates under a limited set of constraints and capabilities.

- **General AI**: Also known as Strong AI, this form of AI would outperform humans at nearly every cognitive task. It is a type of AI that doesn't yet exist but would be capable of thinking, understanding, and acting in a way that is indistinguishable from a human.

- **Artificial Superintelligence**: A hypothetical AI that not only mimics but surpasses human abilities, potentially leading to an era where AI could enhance itself to create even more advanced generations of AI.

How AI Works

- **Machine Learning**: The most common method in AI, machine learning involves algorithms learning from data, identifying patterns, and making decisions with minimal human intervention. Examples include recommendation systems like those on Netflix or Amazon.

- **Deep Learning**: A subset of machine learning, deep learning uses neural networks with three or more layers. These networks can learn from vast amounts of unstructured data, such as images, sound, and text.
- **Natural Language Processing (NLP)**: NLP enables machines to understand and interpret human language. It powers technologies such as chatbots and voice-operated GPS devices.

Applications of AI

- **Everyday Applications:** From the personal assistants on our smartphones, like Siri and Google Assistant, to more sophisticated applications such as fraud detection systems in banking, AI's applications are vast and varied.
- **Future Potential:** As AI technology continues to advance, its potential applications seem almost limitless, promising even greater impacts on society, economy, and daily life.

Key Takeaways

This introduction to AI not only clarifies what AI is and how it functions but also sets the stage for understanding its practical applications, especially in personal finance. By grasping the basics and types of AI, readers can better appreciate the discussions on AI tools for credit improvement in later chapters, where the focus shifts to specific technologies aiding personal financial management.

2.2 How AI Is Changing Industries

Artificial Intelligence (AI) is not just a technological advancement; it is a paradigm shift affecting numerous sectors globally. This section explores how AI is driving change across various industries, focusing on its transformative impact and the innovations it enables.

Transformative Impact Across Sectors

- **Healthcare**: AI is revolutionizing healthcare by improving diagnostic accuracy, personalizing treatment plans, and optimizing hospital operations. Machine learning algorithms can analyze complex medical data faster than human providers, leading to earlier and more accurate diagnoses. AI-driven robots assist in surgeries with precision beyond human capabilities, enhancing patient outcomes.

- **Automotive**: The automotive industry is being transformed by AI through the development of autonomous vehicles. AI systems process information from vehicle sensors and external data to make split-second decisions that can navigate roads safely and efficiently. This technology promises to reduce accidents, improve traffic flow, and decrease carbon emissions.

- **Retail**: In the retail sector, AI enhances customer experiences and streamlines operations. From personalized shopping recommendations based on browsing and purchase history to inventory management systems that predict product demand, AI helps retailers meet consumer needs more effectively and increase operational efficiency.

- **Finance**: AI dramatically changes how financial institutions operate, offering automated trading, risk assessment, and fraud detection. Chatbots and AI-driven interfaces provide personalized customer service, making financial advice more accessible. AI's ability to analyze large volumes of data enhances decision-making in lending, investment, and customer relationship management.

AI's Role in Personalizing Services

- **Personalization at Scale**: AI excels in delivering personalized experiences to large numbers of users simultaneously. For example, streaming services like Netflix use AI to analyze viewing habits and tailor content recommendations to individual tastes.

- **Customer Interaction**: AI technologies, especially those using natural language processing, have transformed how businesses interact with customers. They provide 24/7 customer service, handle inquiries, and resolve issues promptly, improving customer satisfaction and loyalty.

Enhancing Efficiency and Reducing Costs

- **Operational Efficiency**: AI optimizes operations by automating routine tasks, which saves time and reduces human error. In industries like manufacturing, AI-powered robots perform precise and repetitive tasks, allowing human workers to focus on more complex problem-solving activities.

- **Cost Reduction**: By automating processes and optimizing resource use, AI helps businesses reduce operational costs. In sectors like energy, AI algorithms predict demand and adjust supply, significantly cutting energy waste and costs.

Key Takeaways

AI's impact on industries is profound and wide-ranging. It not only enhances efficiency and personalizes services but also opens up new opportunities for innovation and growth. Understanding these changes is crucial for anticipating future trends and recognizing the potential of AI to revolutionize personal finance, particularly in areas like credit management, which will be explored further in subsequent chapters. This backdrop sets the stage for a deeper discussion on how AI can be directly utilized to improve personal credit scores and overall financial health.

2.3 AI in Personal Finance: A Primer

As Artificial Intelligence (AI) transforms various industries, its integration into personal finance is particularly significant, enhancing how individuals manage their money, improve their credit scores, and make financial decisions. This section introduces how AI is applied in personal finance, providing a primer on its benefits and functionalities in this domain.

Enhancing Credit Scoring and Management

- **Advanced Credit Scoring Models:** AI algorithms incorporate a wider range of data points, including rental payment histories, utility bill payments, and even social media activities, to provide a more comprehensive assessment of creditworthiness. This holistic approach can help individuals, especially those with thin credit files or recovering from financial setbacks, improve their credit scores.

- **Real-Time Credit Monitoring**: AI-powered tools continuously monitor credit reports for changes or unusual activities, quickly alerting users to potential errors or fraudulent transactions. This prompt response helps in maintaining accurate credit files and protecting credit health.

Streamlining Debt Management

- **Personalized Repayment Plans:** AI analyzes an individual's financial situation, including income, expenses, and existing debts, to create optimized repayment strategies. These tools can suggest the most effective ways to allocate funds across different debts, potentially reducing interest payments and shortening debt cycles.

- **Automated Negotiation Tools:** Some AI platforms can negotiate with creditors on behalf of users to lower interest rates or settle debts under more favorable terms. These tools use vast data sets to simulate negotiation strategies and predict creditor responses.

Budgeting and Financial Planning

- **Smart Budgeting Tools:** AI helps individuals manage their finances by tracking spending patterns and suggesting budgets that align with their financial goals. These tools can also forecast future spending needs based on past behavior, aiding in more accurate and sustainable financial planning.

- **Investment Advice:** Robo-advisors are AI-driven platforms that provide personalized investment advice at a lower cost than human advisors. They analyze market data to offer tailored investment strategies based on an individual's risk tolerance and financial goals.

Fraud Detection and Prevention

- **Enhanced Security:** AI systems are crucial in detecting and preventing fraud. They analyze behavioral patterns to identify anomalous transactions that may indicate fraud, significantly faster than traditional methods. This capability is vital in protecting individuals' financial assets and information.

Key Takeaways

AI's role in personal finance is multifaceted, addressing everything from credit management to budgeting and investments. By automating routine tasks and providing data-driven insights and recommendations, AI empowers individuals to make more informed financial decisions. This primer sets the stage for deeper exploration into specific AI tools and strategies that can be utilized to directly improve credit scores and overall financial well-being, as will be discussed in the upcoming chapters. This understanding of AI's potential in personal finance not only broadens one's perspective on managing personal finances but also illustrates practical ways AI can enhance financial stability and independence.

PART II
AI Tools for Credit Improvement

In this section of the book, we delve into the specific AI tools designed to enhance credit management. From monitoring and improving credit scores to managing debt and optimizing financial behaviors, AI technologies offer powerful solutions that can transform your financial health. Each chapter is dedicated to different aspects of credit improvement, providing insights into how AI can be utilized to make strategic financial decisions and improve creditworthiness.

Chapter 3: Monitoring Your Credit with AI

- **Real-Time Credit Monitoring:** Explore AI tools that continuously monitor credit reports, detecting errors, inconsistencies, and fraudulent activities quickly. Understand how these tools work and the benefits of keeping a vigilant eye on your credit status.

- **Predictive Analytics for Credit Health:** Discuss how AI uses predictive analytics to forecast potential issues with your credit score and provides proactive recommendations to prevent them.

- **Case Studies:** Highlight successful case studies where individuals used AI credit monitoring tools to significantly enhance their credit scores and detect potential fraud before it caused damage.

Chapter 4: AI and Debt Management

- **AI-Driven Debt Repayment Plans:** Learn about AI systems that analyze your financial data to create personalized debt repayment strategies, focusing on optimizing payments to minimize interest and reduce balance faster.

- **Automated Negotiation Tools:** Detail how AI can automate negotiations with creditors for better interest rates or favorable repayment terms, backed by data-driven tactics and scenarios.

- **Impact Assessment:** Review how these tools impact an individual's overall financial health by comparing before and after scenarios of AI-integrated debt management.

Chapter 5: Budgeting with AI

- **Intelligent Budgeting Tools**: Examine AI applications that assist in creating and maintaining effective budgets. See how these tools analyze spending habits, income stability, and financial goals to suggest optimal budget plans.

- **Forecasting Financial Needs**: Discuss how AI can predict future financial scenarios based on current trends, helping users plan for upcoming expenses and avoid overextending their finances.

- **Success Stories**: Share examples of how real people have successfully utilized AI budgeting tools to stay on track with their financial goals, reduce wasteful spending, and improve their credit scores.

Chapter 6: Improving Credit Scores with AI

- **Enhancing Credit Score Algorithms**: Explore how AI enhances traditional credit scoring models by incorporating non-traditional data sources and learning from consumer behavior patterns over time.

- **AI Recommendations for Credit Improvement**: Provide practical tips and strategies suggested by AI tools that users can implement to improve their credit scores, such as optimal credit utilization rates and timely payment strategies.

- **Evaluating Credit Score Changes**: Analyze how AI-driven changes to credit management practices can lead to substantial improvements in credit scores over time.

Key Takeaways

This section of the book is designed to give readers a comprehensive understanding of the various AI tools available for credit improvement. By the end of Part II, readers should be equipped with the knowledge of how these tools function, the benefits they offer, and how to integrate them into their personal financial management strategies. Through practical examples and case studies, this section not only educates but also inspires readers to take proactive steps towards using AI to secure a healthier financial future.

03
Monitoring Your Credit with AI

In today's digital age, keeping a vigilant eye on your credit is crucial. This chapter explores how AI-powered tools can significantly enhance the monitoring of your credit report, detecting errors, inconsistencies, and potential fraud with unprecedented accuracy and speed. We will delve into the functionalities of these tools, their benefits, and how they can be a game-changer in managing and improving your credit score.

Real-Time Credit Monitoring

- **Overview of Tools**: Introduce the leading AI-driven credit monitoring tools available in the market. Explain how these tools integrate with credit reporting agencies and personal finance data to provide continuous surveillance.

- **How It Works**: Describe the technical process behind AI's real-time monitoring capabilities, including data collection, pattern recognition, and anomaly detection. Discuss how AI algorithms are trained to recognize typical user behavior and flag deviations that could indicate errors or fraud.

- **Benefits**: Highlight the advantages of using AI for credit monitoring, such as early detection of identity theft, quick correction of report errors, and the peace of mind that comes with knowing your credit status is being watched over 24/7.

Predictive Analytics for Credit Health

- **Predictive Capabilities:** Explain how AI uses historical data and statistical algorithms to predict future credit behavior and potential risks. Illustrate this with examples of how predictive analytics can forecast dips in credit scores based on spending patterns or financial commitments.

- **Proactive Recommendations:** Discuss how AI tools not only monitor and predict but also provide actionable recommendations to prevent credit score deterioration. For example, if a predicted cash flow problem might lead to late payments, the AI tool could advise earlier corrective actions like adjusting spending or consolidating debts.

- **Customization and Learning:** Detail how these AI systems adapt to individual financial behaviors over time, improving their predictive accuracy and making personalized recommendations more relevant and effective.

Case Studies

- **Success Stories:** Present a series of case studies where individuals utilized AI monitoring tools to detect and resolve credit issues, leading to substantial improvements in their credit scores. These stories will illustrate the practical application and tangible benefits of AI in credit monitoring.

- **Industry Applications:** Share examples from financial institutions that have implemented AI monitoring tools to enhance customer service and fraud prevention, further demonstrating the technology's reliability and effectiveness.

Challenges and Considerations

- **Privacy and Security Concerns:** Address potential concerns about data privacy and security related to using AI tools for credit monitoring. Discuss the measures taken by tool providers to protect user data and comply with regulatory standards.

- **Limitations of AI:** While AI can significantly enhance credit monitoring, it's important to discuss its limitations. For instance, AI may not always interpret context as accurately as a human might, which can lead to false alarms or overlooked issues.

Key Takeaways

By the end of this chapter, readers will understand the critical role of AI in modern credit monitoring, equipped with knowledge about the most effective tools and how they can be utilized to safeguard and improve their credit score. The discussion aims to empower readers to make informed decisions about incorporating AI-driven monitoring into their personal finance management, enhancing their ability to maintain a healthy credit profile in an increasingly digital world.

3.1 How AI Monitors Credit

AI-driven credit monitoring represents a significant advancement in personal finance management. This section explains how AI technologies are employed to monitor credit, detailing the processes involved and the benefits of using such systems. Understanding these mechanisms is crucial for anyone looking to leverage AI for maintaining or improving their credit score.

Overview of AI Credit Monitoring Tools

- **Tool Functionality**: Begin by outlining the typical features of AI credit monitoring tools. These can include automatic alerts, regular credit report updates, and personalized insights based on credit activity.

- **Key Players**: Introduce some of the leading AI credit monitoring tools available in the market, such as those offered by major credit bureaus, fintech startups, and personal finance apps.

Technical Process of AI Monitoring

- **Data Collection**: Explain how AI tools gather data from various sources including credit bureaus, banks, and public records. This data forms the basis for all subsequent analyses.

- **Pattern Recognition**: Discuss how machine learning algorithms are used to recognize patterns in credit usage, payment history, and even potential errors or inconsistencies in credit reports. These patterns help the AI identify what is normal and what could be a sign of something amiss, such as potential fraud or identity theft.

- **Anomaly Detection**: Describe how AI tools use statistical techniques to detect anomalies that deviate from established patterns. For instance, a sudden spike in credit utilization or multiple credit inquiries in a short period might trigger an alert.

- **Continuous Learning**: Highlight how AI systems continuously learn and adapt from new data. As a user's financial behavior changes over time, the AI refines its understanding, improving its predictive accuracy and the relevance of the alerts it generates.

Benefits of AI in Credit Monitoring

- **Proactive Fraud Detection**: Emphasize the role of AI in detecting fraudulent activities faster than traditional methods. By constantly analyzing transaction data and spotting irregularities, AI tools can alert users to potential fraud before significant damage is done.

- **Error Correction**: Explain how AI can help users spot and rectify errors in their credit reports. AI tools can identify discrepancies such as incorrect account information or duplicated entries, which can then be disputed to improve credit accuracy.

- **Real-Time Alerts**: Discuss the benefit of receiving real-time alerts about significant changes to one's credit report. This immediate feedback allows users to act swiftly in case of problems, whether it's addressing a mistaken penalty on their credit or responding to a fraudulent charge.

User Empowerment Through Customization

- **Personalized Insights**: Detail how AI tools not only monitor but also analyze credit data to provide personalized advice. For example, if an AI tool notices high credit utilization, it may suggest strategies to reduce it or offer recommendations for debt consolidation.

- **Setting Preferences**: Illustrate how users can customize the types of alerts they receive, allowing them to focus on specific aspects of their credit or financial activity that they are most concerned about.

Key Takeaways

AI-powered credit monitoring tools offer an advanced, efficient, and user-friendly way to keep an eye on one's financial activities and credit health. They provide crucial alerts that can prevent fraud, assist in managing credit more effectively, and help maintain a healthy credit score. This section helps demystify the technology behind AI monitoring and demonstrates its practical benefits, empowering readers to take proactive steps in safeguarding their financial future.

3.2 Best AI Tools for Credit Monitoring

In this section, we'll explore some of the most effective AI-powered tools available for credit monitoring. These tools leverage advanced technologies to provide users with real-time alerts, personalized insights, and proactive management of their credit profiles. Here's an overview of the leading solutions in the market, highlighting their unique features and how they can help users maintain and improve their credit scores.

Leading AI Credit Monitoring Tools

1. **Credit Karma**
    - **Features**: Offers free credit scores, reports, and monitoring, along with personalized advice on how to improve your credit. Uses AI to analyze your financial data and suggest the best credit cards and loans based on your credit score.

- **Benefits**: Besides monitoring, it provides tools for error reporting directly to credit bureaus and simulates how your credit score could change with different financial decisions.

2. **Experian Boost**
   - **Features**: Allows users to improve their credit scores instantly by adding utility and telecom bill payments to their credit file. Uses AI to scan your bank account data for qualifying payments and updates your credit file almost in real time.
   - **Benefits**: Particularly beneficial for those with thin credit files or low scores, as it can provide an immediate boost by considering alternative data.

3. **Mint by Intuit**
   - **Features**: Provides credit monitoring along with budgeting tools. Mint uses AI to analyze your transactions, categorize your spending, and provide tailored financial advice.
   - **Benefits**: Integrates credit monitoring with overall financial management, offering a holistic approach to personal finance.

4. **IdentityForce**
   - **Features**: Includes advanced credit and identity theft protection. Utilizes AI-driven analytics to monitor, alert, and help remediate identity theft, including credit-related issues.

- o **Benefits:** Offers robust monitoring of personal information, including social security numbers, and provides alerts if your information is compromised.

5. **myFICO**
   - o **Features:** Offers detailed FICO score reports from all three bureaus. The platform uses AI to provide score analysis and explain the factors that are affecting your score.
   - o **Benefits:** Focused on FICO scores, which are used by a majority of lenders, providing a clear insight into the specific scores that will impact loan and credit approvals.

How to Choose the Right Tool

- **Consider Your Needs:** Determine whether you need simple credit monitoring, identity theft protection, or a more comprehensive financial management tool.
- **Evaluate Features:** Look for tools that provide real-time alerts, a user-friendly interface, and insightful reporting. Consider if you can benefit from features like score simulators or identity theft insurance.
- **Check Compatibility:** Ensure that the tool integrates well with your bank and credit accounts and that it supports all necessary platforms (iOS, Android, web).
- **Read Reviews:** User reviews can provide valuable insights into the effectiveness of the tool, the quality of customer service, and the user experience.

Key Takeaways

Choosing the right AI tool for credit monitoring can significantly affect your ability to manage your credit effectively. These tools not only provide essential alerts and insights but also empower you to take proactive steps toward improving your credit score. By integrating one of these AI solutions into your financial strategy, you can maintain better control over your credit health and make more informed decisions about your finances.

3.3 Setting Up Alerts and Notifications

Effective credit monitoring involves not just passive observation, but active management of your financial activities. Alerts and notifications play a crucial role in this process, enabling you to respond promptly to changes in your credit report or potential threats to your financial stability. This section will guide you through setting up and optimizing alerts and notifications with AI credit monitoring tools, ensuring you're always informed and ready to act when necessary.

Understanding Alert Types

- **Credit Inquiry Alerts**: Receive notifications whenever there is a new inquiry on your credit report, such as when a lender checks your credit for a loan or credit card application. This helps in identifying unauthorized inquiries and potential fraud.

- **Account Balance Updates**: Set alerts for changes in your account balances that could affect your credit utilization rate, a critical factor in your credit score.

- **Score Change Alerts**: Get notified when your credit score changes. This is vital for tracking your credit health and understanding how your financial behaviors influence your score.

- **Fraud Alerts:** Some AI tools offer specialized notifications for suspicious activities, like unexpected account openings or credit applications, which could indicate identity theft.

How to Set Up Alerts

1. **Choose a Credit Monitoring Tool:** Select a tool that offers comprehensive monitoring services and customizable alerts. Refer to section 3.2 for suggestions on selecting a tool that fits your needs.

2. **Register and Verify Your Accounts:** Sign up and connect your financial accounts to the tool. This often involves verifying your identity and linking bank accounts, credit cards, and loans to ensure comprehensive monitoring.

3. **Customize Your Alert Settings:** Most tools offer customizable alert settings. You can choose what types of notifications you receive and how you receive them (e.g., email, text messages, app notifications). It's important to prioritize alerts that match your specific concerns and financial situation.

4. **Review and Adjust:** As you start receiving alerts, review them to ensure they are helpful and adjust the settings if needed. For example, if you find that certain alerts are too frequent or not useful, you might tweak the settings to make them more relevant.

Best Practices for Managing Alerts

- **Regular Updates:** As your financial situation evolves, update your settings to match new priorities or accounts.

- **Immediate Action:** Always take immediate action on alerts that suggest unauthorized access or potential fraud. This may involve contacting your financial institution, changing passwords, or placing a freeze on your credit.

- **Educate Yourself:** Understand the implications of different types of alerts. Some AI tools offer educational resources to help you interpret and respond to notifications appropriately.

Key Takeaways

Properly set up alerts and notifications are essential tools for proactive credit management. They not only keep you informed about important changes in your financial profile but also empower you to take immediate actions to safeguard your credit health. By leveraging AI-driven tools to customize and manage these alerts, you can maintain a vigilant watch over your financial activities and react swiftly to any potential issues. This proactive approach is key to maintaining a healthy credit score and securing your financial future.

04
AI and Debt Management

Effective debt management is crucial for maintaining and improving your credit score. This chapter explores how Artificial Intelligence (AI) can aid in this critical area, offering sophisticated tools that automate and optimize debt repayment strategies. By leveraging AI, individuals can navigate their debts more efficiently and strategically, potentially saving money and enhancing their credit profiles over time.

AI-Driven Debt Repayment Plans

- **Personalized Repayment Strategies**: AI tools analyze your entire financial situation—including income, expenses, debts, and personal savings goals—to create customized debt repayment plans. These plans prioritize debts based on interest rates, balances, and the potential impact on your credit score, suggesting which debts to pay off first to maximize financial efficiency.

- **Automated Payments**: Some AI platforms offer the ability to set up automated payments that align with these strategies, ensuring that payments are made on time and are optimized for debt reduction without manual oversight.

- **Benefits**: Users can see reduced interest payments and quicker debt reduction, along with improvements in their credit scores due to better debt management and fewer missed payments.

Automated Negotiation Tools

- **Creditor Negotiations**: AI tools can also simulate and execute negotiations with creditors for lower interest rates or more favorable repayment terms. These tools use large datasets to understand which negotiation strategies are most likely to succeed based on creditor histories and the specific circumstances of the debtor.

- **Settlement Services**: For those in severe debt, AI can help identify opportunities for debt settlement. AI analyzes whether settling a debt versus paying in full will be more beneficial in the long-term financial context of the user.

- **Impact on Credit Score**: While negotiating debt terms can sometimes impact your credit score temporarily, AI tools also provide insights on how these negotiations affect your credit in the long run and how to mitigate any negative effects.

Integrating AI into Budgeting for Debt Management

- **Budget Optimization for Debt Repayment**: AI tools integrate debt repayment into overall budgeting, adjusting monthly spending categories to free up more funds for debt elimination without sacrificing essential expenses.

- **Forecasting Future Financial Scenarios**: AI can forecast future cash flows based on current income and spending patterns, helping to predict how changes in spending or debt repayment will affect overall financial health.

- **Real-time Adjustments**: AI systems can suggest real-time adjustments to spending or repayment plans based on unexpected financial changes, such as a sudden expense or a change in income.

Case Studies and Real-World Applications

- **Success Stories:** Provide real-life examples of individuals who have successfully used AI-driven tools to manage and reduce their debt. These stories can illustrate the practical benefits and possible challenges encountered during the process.

- **Comparative Analysis:** Compare scenarios with and without AI assistance, highlighting the effectiveness and impact of AI in managing debts more efficiently.

Key Takeaways

AI's role in debt management opens up new avenues for consumers to handle their financial obligations more intelligently and proactively. By utilizing AI tools for debt repayment planning, negotiation, and budget integration, individuals can significantly enhance their ability to manage debts, reduce financial stress, and improve their credit scores. This chapter equips readers with the knowledge and tools necessary to leverage AI in transforming their approach to debt management, ultimately leading to better financial health and freedom.

4.1 AI in Debt Repayment Strategies

Debt repayment is a critical aspect of financial management, impacting credit scores and overall financial health. Artificial Intelligence (AI) offers sophisticated tools that can personalize and optimize debt repayment strategies. This section explores how AI can analyze financial data and user behaviors to devise effective debt repayment plans tailored to individual needs.

Understanding AI-Driven Debt Repayment Plans

- **Data Utilization**: AI systems start by aggregating and analyzing extensive data on an individual's financial situation, including income, debts, monthly expenses, and spending habits. This comprehensive overview allows AI to identify the most effective strategies for debt repayment.

- **Debt Prioritization**: Using principles from debt repayment strategies like the debt snowball (paying off debts from smallest to largest balance) and debt avalanche (targeting debts with the highest interest rates first), AI can prioritize debts in a way that saves interest over time and can more quickly improve credit scores.

- **Customization**: AI algorithms adapt these strategies based on user preferences—for example, focusing on quickly freeing up monthly cash flow or minimizing total interest paid.

Benefits of AI in Debt Repayment

- **Efficiency**: AI can quickly calculate the optimal payment amounts for each debt account, taking into account the impact of different strategies on the overall financial picture.

- **Personalization**: Unlike one-size-fits-all approaches, AI provides personalized recommendations that consider an individual's unique financial goals and circumstances.

- **Dynamism**: AI systems can adjust recommendations based on changes in financial status, such as an increase in income or unexpected expenses, ensuring that debt repayment plans remain realistic and effective.

Implementing AI-Driven Debt Repayment Plans

- **Tool Integration:** Most personal finance management tools that utilize AI for debt repayment require users to link their financial accounts for real-time data syncing. This integration allows the AI to continuously monitor and adjust recommendations based on up-to-date information.

- **User Interaction:** Users can often interact with AI tools via mobile apps or web platforms, where they can view their repayment plans, track progress, and receive notifications about upcoming payments or strategy adjustments.

- **Automated Payments:** Some AI tools offer the option to automate debt payments according to the devised strategy, ensuring payments are always made on time, which is crucial for credit health.

Real-World Examples and Case Studies

- **Case Study 1:** An individual with multiple credit card debts and a personal loan utilizes an AI tool to implement a debt avalanche strategy. The AI's analysis shows that by reallocating monthly payments to target the highest interest rates first, the individual could save thousands in interest and shorten the debt repayment period by several months.

- **Case Study 2:** A user facing cash flow issues opts for a debt snowball strategy recommended by an AI tool, leading to quick wins by clearing smaller debts, which significantly improves their motivation and credit score.

Key Takeaways

AI-driven debt repayment strategies can transform the way individuals manage their debts, offering more efficient, personalized, and adaptable solutions. By leveraging the power of AI, users can not only accelerate their debt repayment but also achieve substantial savings in interest, ultimately enhancing their financial freedom and creditworthiness. This section highlights the potential of AI to revolutionize debt management through tailored advice and automated solutions.

4.2 Prioritizing Your Debts with AI

Effectively managing and prioritizing debt repayment can significantly impact your financial stability and credit health. AI technology plays a crucial role in analyzing various debt factors and advising on the optimal sequence for repayment. This section explores how AI helps to strategize debt repayment by prioritizing debts based on interest rates, balances, and potential impacts on your credit score.

Importance of Debt Prioritization

- **Financial Efficiency**: Prioritizing debts correctly can reduce the amount of interest paid over time, thus saving money.
- **Credit Score Impact**: Proper debt management, including timely and strategic repayments, can improve or maintain a good credit score by demonstrating responsible credit usage and reliability to lenders.

How AI Prioritizes Debts

- **Assessment of Debt Profiles:** AI tools start by gathering comprehensive data on all your debts, including types of debt (credit card, mortgage, student loans, etc.), interest rates, balances, and terms.

- **Interest Rate Analysis:** The AI evaluates which debts have the highest interest rates, which are typically prioritized to reduce the total interest paid over the life of the debts.

- **Balance Considerations:** For some strategies, like the debt snowball method, the AI may suggest paying off smaller balances first to create psychological wins that motivate continued debt repayment efforts.

- **Credit Impact Modeling:** AI uses predictive models to estimate how different repayment strategies affect your credit score. For example, paying off high-utilization credit cards first might be recommended to improve your credit score more quickly.

Integrating AI Recommendations into Financial Plans

- **Personalized Strategy Development:** Based on your financial goals (e.g., improving credit score, minimizing interest payments), AI tools suggest personalized repayment plans. Users can adjust their priorities, like focusing on short-term credit score improvements for an upcoming loan application.

- **Dynamic Adjustment Capability:** AI systems continuously update and adjust recommendations based on changes in your financial situation, such as a change in income or unexpected expenses.

- **User Interaction and Feedback:** Most AI debt management tools allow users to provide feedback on recommended strategies, which the AI uses to refine future recommendations, making the tool more responsive and effective over time.

Practical Application and Tools

- **Case Study Example:** A case study where an individual used an AI tool to restructure $30,000 in mixed debt. The tool prioritized high-interest credit cards and suggested extra payments when the user's monthly income increased, significantly reducing the debt payoff time.

- **Recommended Tools:** Examples of popular AI-powered financial management tools include Mint, YNAB (You Need A Budget), and Tally. Each tool offers different features tailored to debt management and prioritization.

Challenges and Considerations

- **Understanding AI Limitations:** While AI provides powerful insights, users need to understand that it relies on the input data's accuracy and completeness.

- **Privacy and Security:** When using AI tools, consider the security of your financial data. Ensure that any tool you use complies with relevant data protection regulations and offers robust security measures.

Key Takeaways

AI's ability to analyze and prioritize debts offers a tailored approach to debt management that can accelerate the journey to financial freedom.

By leveraging AI to make informed decisions about debt repayment, individuals can not only save on interest but also potentially boost their credit scores, enhancing their overall financial health. This section empowers readers with knowledge of how AI tools work in the background to optimize debt repayment strategies and what factors they need to consider when using these tools.

4.3 Success Stories: AI and Debt Reduction

Personal testimonials and success stories can vividly illustrate the real-world impact of AI on debt management. This section showcases several case studies where individuals successfully utilized AI tools to reduce their debts significantly. These stories highlight the practical benefits of AI in debt management, providing inspiration and actionable insights for readers.

Case Study 1: Overcoming Credit Card Debt

- **Background:** Sarah, a graphic designer, struggled with $15,000 in credit card debt across multiple cards, accruing high interest.

- **AI Solution:** She used an AI-driven debt management app that analyzed her financial data and recommended a debt avalanche strategy, prioritizing her highest interest debts.

- **Outcome:** Within 18 months, Sarah not only reduced her debt by 70% but also improved her credit score by over 100 points. The AI tool provided her with monthly updates and adjustments based on her spending habits and additional freelance income.

Case Study 2: Student Loan Management

- **Background**: James, a recent college graduate, faced $25,000 in student loans with varying interest rates.

- **AI Solution**: He utilized an AI tool that consolidated his loans and calculated an optimized payment plan, factoring in his entry-level job salary.

- **Outcome**: The tool helped James adjust his repayment plan dynamically as his salary increased, allowing him to pay off his loans five years earlier than expected, saving thousands in interest.

Case Study 3: Small Business Debt Resolution

- **Background**: Maria, a small business owner, accumulated debt to maintain her business operations during an economic downturn.

- **AI Solution**: An AI platform helped Maria restructure her business debts based on projected cash flows and prioritized repayment to creditors posing the highest financial risk.

- **Outcome**: Maria was able to avoid bankruptcy, stabilize her business, and return to profitability within two years. The AI tool continuously adapted to her changing financial circumstances, providing ongoing support.

Case Study 4: Automating Savings and Debt Payments

- **Background**: Tom, an IT professional, often missed opportunities to save or make extra payments towards his mortgage due to a hectic schedule.

- **AI Solution:** He adopted an AI personal finance assistant that automatically identified surplus funds each month and applied them to his mortgage principal.

- **Outcome:** Tom reduced his mortgage term by seven years and saved substantially on interest, all without having to manually manage his payments or savings.

Analysis and Key Takeaways

- **Common Themes:** These stories highlight several recurring themes, such as the importance of personalized strategies, the benefits of dynamic adjustments based on life changes, and the role of AI in providing psychological encouragement and discipline.

- **Practical Benefits:** Each case demonstrates practical benefits, including significant savings on interest, improved credit scores, and in some cases, the prevention of bankruptcy.

- **User Engagement:** Success often depended not only on the technology itself but also on the users' engagement with the AI recommendations and their commitment to follow through on the advice given.

Conclusion

These success stories underscore the transformative potential of AI in managing and reducing debt. By leveraging AI tools, individuals can gain control over their financial destinies, making smarter decisions that lead to real economic benefits. This section not only motivates readers with real success but also provides a blueprint for how AI can be a powerful ally in the journey toward financial freedom.

05
Budgeting with AI

Effective budgeting is essential for financial stability and growth, and Artificial Intelligence (AI) has revolutionized this aspect of personal finance. This chapter explores how AI can help individuals create, maintain, and optimize their budgets, enhancing their ability to manage finances more efficiently and achieve financial goals faster.

AI-Driven Budgeting Tools

- **Overview of Tools:** Introduce the leading AI-powered budgeting tools such as Mint, YNAB (You Need A Budget), and PocketGuard, highlighting their unique features and how they utilize AI to aid in financial management.

- **Functionality:** Discuss how these tools use AI to automatically categorize transactions, track spending habits, and provide real-time updates on budget status. This automation reduces the manual effort required and increases accuracy in tracking.

How AI Enhances Budgeting

- **Personalized Budget Creation:** AI analyzes past spending behavior, income fluctuations, and financial goals to create personalized budget plans. These plans are tailored to maximize savings and efficiently allocate funds towards debt repayment and other financial objectives.

- **Proactive Adjustments**: AI tools continually monitor financial activity and can suggest adjustments to the budget based on real-time data. For instance, if unexpected expenses occur, AI can recommend temporary cuts in other budget categories to compensate.
- **Goal Setting and Tracking**: AI enhances goal setting by providing realistic, data-driven targets for savings and spending. It also tracks progress towards these goals, offering motivational feedback and alerts to keep users on track.

Case Studies and Practical Applications

- **Case Study 1**: A family uses an AI budgeting tool to manage their household expenses. The tool helps them identify unnecessary expenditures, optimize grocery spending, and allocate more funds towards their children's education fund.
- **Case Study 2**: An individual uses AI to adjust his budget dynamically as he transitions from a full-time job to freelancing. The AI tool helps manage irregular income streams and variable expenses, ensuring financial stability during the transition.

Integrating AI into Everyday Financial Decisions

- **Daily Spending Decisions**: AI can provide daily or weekly spending limits based on overall financial health and goals. This helps individuals make informed decisions about discretionary spending.
- **Forecasting Future Expenses**: AI tools can predict future financial scenarios based on seasonal spending trends and

upcoming financial obligations, allowing users to prepare in advance and adjust their budgets accordingly.

- **Financial Health Overview:** AI budgeting tools often provide a comprehensive view of one's financial health, incorporating elements like net worth calculations, debt-to-income ratios, and savings rates, which are crucial for long-term financial planning.

Challenges and Ethical Considerations

- **Privacy Concerns:** Discuss the implications of sharing personal financial data with AI platforms, including how data is stored, used, and protected.

- **Dependence on Technology:** Address potential issues related to over-reliance on AI for financial decision-making, emphasizing the importance of maintaining personal oversight and understanding of one's financial situation.

Key Takeaways

AI-powered budgeting tools offer a revolutionary approach to managing personal finances, providing significant advantages in terms of efficiency, personalization, and proactive financial management. By leveraging AI, individuals can not only maintain tighter control over their budgets but also make smarter financial decisions that pave the way toward achieving their financial goals. This chapter aims to equip readers with the knowledge and tools necessary to effectively integrate AI into their budgeting practices, transforming the way they approach personal finance.

5.1 AI Budgeting Tools: An Overview

In the realm of personal finance, budgeting is a fundamental task that can benefit greatly from advancements in technology. AI budgeting tools bring a level of automation and insight that was previously unavailable, making it easier for individuals to manage their finances efficiently. This section provides an overview of AI budgeting tools, detailing how they work, their key features, and the benefits they offer.

Introduction to AI Budgeting Tools

AI budgeting tools leverage artificial intelligence to help users manage their personal finances by automating the categorization of expenses, forecasting future spending, and offering personalized financial advice. These tools are designed to integrate seamlessly into everyday life, providing real-time financial insights and proactive budget management.

Key Features of AI Budgeting Tools

- **Automatic Transaction Categorization**: AI algorithms can automatically categorize transactions as they occur, which helps users track where their money is going without the need for manual entry.

- **Spending Insights and Trends**: By analyzing past transactions, AI tools can identify spending trends and habits, providing users with insights that can help them adjust their spending behaviors.

- **Budget Creation and Adjustment**: AI tools assist in setting up budgets based on past spending and financial goals. They can also adjust budgets dynamically in response to changes in income or unexpected expenses.

- **Goal Setting and Progress Tracking**: Users can set financial goals (such as saving for a vacation or paying off debt) within these tools, and AI will track progress and suggest adjustments to meet these goals more effectively.

- **Alerts and Notifications**: These tools send alerts for important financial events, such as approaching the limit of a budget category, large transactions, or upcoming bills, ensuring users can react in a timely manner.

Examples of Popular AI Budgeting Tools

- **Mint**: One of the most well-known financial management tools, Mint offers features like bill tracking, budgeting, and personalized insights based on spending patterns, all powered by AI.

- **YNAB (You Need A Budget)**: YNAB focuses on budgeting to give every dollar a job. Its AI-driven approach helps users allocate funds effectively to reduce debt and build savings.

- **PocketGuard**: This app uses AI to analyze your spending habits and income to create an "in my pocket" balance, showing how much money you can safely spend while still adhering to your budget.

- **Toshl Finance**: Toshl incorporates AI to connect with various financial accounts, track expenses, and project future spending, making it easier to understand financial standing and plan ahead.

Benefits of Using AI Budgeting Tools

- **Time Efficiency**: Automation of routine financial management tasks saves time and reduces the likelihood of errors associated with manual budgeting.

- **Improved Financial Awareness**: Continuous monitoring and insights help users understand their financial habits better, promoting more informed spending and saving decisions.

- **Enhanced Financial Planning**: With predictive analytics, these tools can forecast future financial scenarios, helping users plan for both short-term expenses and long-term financial goals.

- **Reduced Financial Stress**: By providing a clear picture of financial health and automating financial planning, AI tools can help alleviate anxiety related to money management.

Key Takeaways

AI budgeting tools are transforming personal finance management by providing powerful, user-friendly solutions that automate and optimize budgeting processes. By understanding and utilizing these tools, individuals can improve their financial literacy and make more strategic decisions that enhance their financial stability and future growth. This overview sets the stage for a deeper exploration of specific AI tools and how they can be integrated into daily financial routines to achieve personal finance goals.

5.2 How to Set Up an AI-Driven Budget

Setting up an AI-driven budget can streamline your financial management, ensuring that you stay on top of your finances with minimal effort. This section will guide you through the process of establishing a budget using AI tools, from selecting the right tool to integrating it into your daily financial routine.

Selecting the Right AI Budgeting Tool

- **Assess Your Needs**: Determine what features are most important to you, such as expense tracking, debt management, savings goals, or investment monitoring.

- **Research and Compare Tools**: Look into popular AI budgeting tools like Mint, YNAB, and PocketGuard. Compare their features, ease of use, security measures, and user reviews.

- **Consider Integration Capabilities**: Ensure the tool can integrate smoothly with your financial institutions and other apps you use for comprehensive tracking.

Setting Up Your Budget

- **Sign Up and Secure Your Account**: Create an account with your chosen tool and secure it with a strong password and any additional security features offered, such as two-factor authentication.

- **Connect Your Financial Accounts**: Link your bank accounts, credit cards, loans, and any other financial accounts. The AI uses this data to analyze your financial status and create a baseline for your budget.

- **Define Your Financial Goals**: Clearly define your short-term and long-term financial goals within the tool. These could include saving for a down payment, paying off debt, or building an emergency fund.

- **Customize Your Spending Categories:** While AI can categorize transactions automatically, customizing these categories to fit your spending habits can improve the accuracy of your budget. Adjust categories and set specific budgets for each based on your past spending and financial goals.

Utilizing AI to Optimize Your Budget

- **Monitor and Adjust Automatically:** AI tools continuously analyze your spending and can suggest budget adjustments in real-time. For example, if you consistently underspend in one category, the AI might suggest reallocating those funds to a different category or a savings goal.

- **Set Up Alerts and Notifications:** Enable alerts for critical budgetary events, like nearing a spending limit or upcoming bills. These notifications can help you avoid overspending and stay on track with your financial goals.

- **Review Insights and Reports:** Regularly review the insights and detailed reports generated by the AI. These can provide a deeper understanding of your financial habits and help you identify areas for improvement.

Engaging with Your AI-Driven Budget

- **Regular Check-ins:** Even with AI assistance, regular personal check-ins are crucial. Ensure that the tool's suggestions and automated categorizations align with your actual spending and financial objectives.

- **Feedback Loop:** Most AI systems improve with feedback. Correct any mis-categorizations and provide input when prompted to help the AI learn from its mistakes and refine its accuracy over time.

- **Adapt as Needed**: As your financial situation changes, update your goals and settings in the budgeting tool to reflect new incomes, expenses, or priorities. This keeps your AI-driven budget relevant and effective.

Key Takeaways

An AI-driven budget can significantly enhance your financial management by automating many of the tedious aspects of budgeting and providing personalized insights and recommendations. By following these steps to set up and engage with your AI budgeting tool, you can ensure that your financial planning is as efficient, accurate, and aligned with your goals as possible. This proactive approach to budget management not only simplifies your financial life but also empowers you to achieve your financial objectives more effectively.

5.3 Tips for Maintaining a Budget with AI

Once you have set up an AI-driven budget, maintaining and optimizing it becomes crucial for sustained financial health and achieving your goals. This section provides practical tips on how to effectively maintain a budget with the assistance of AI, ensuring it remains a valuable tool in your financial management toolkit.

Review Regularly

- **Consistent Check-ins:** Regularly review your budget to ensure it aligns with your current financial situation and goals. Monthly or quarterly reviews are recommended.

- **Adapt to Changes:** If there are significant life events, such as a new job, a move, or a change in family size, update your budget to reflect these changes. AI tools can adjust recommendations based on updated information.

Utilize AI for Continuous Learning

- **Feed Accurate Data:** The effectiveness of AI depends on the quality of data it receives. Ensure all transactions are correctly categorized and all financial accounts are linked to the AI tool.

- **Engage with Insights:** Many AI tools provide insights based on your spending patterns and saving habits. Engage with these insights to understand your financial behavior better and make informed decisions.

- **Iterate Based on Feedback:** Use the AI tool's feedback mechanism to correct any inaccuracies in transaction categorization or budget allocation. This helps improve the tool's algorithms and increases the accuracy of its advice over time.

Leverage Notifications and Alerts

- **Set Custom Alerts:** Customize alerts for budget limits, bill due dates, large transactions, or low account balances. These alerts can help prevent overspending and ensure timely bill payments.

- **Respond Promptly**: When you receive an alert, take immediate action if necessary. This could involve transferring funds to avoid overdraft fees or adjusting spending to stay within budget.

Integrate Budgeting into Daily Life

- **Automate Where Possible**: Use the AI tool's features to automate routine financial tasks, such as transferring funds to savings or paying recurring bills. This reduces the manual effort needed and helps avoid late payments.

- **Sync with Your Calendar**: Integrate financial reviews and budget check-ins with your regular scheduling or calendar app. This ensures you do not overlook these important tasks amidst daily activities.

Educate Yourself Continuously

- **Stay Informed**: Keep up with new features and updates in your AI budgeting tool. Software updates may include enhanced functionalities that can offer deeper insights or more efficient management of your finances.

- **Learn from Patterns**: Use the historical data and pattern recognition capabilities of AI to learn from past financial mistakes and successes. Understanding these patterns can help you plan better for future expenses and investments.

Foster Financial Discipline

- **Set Realistic Goals**: Ensure that your financial goals are achievable and realistic. AI can help simulate different scenarios and show you how changing one variable, like saving an extra percentage of your income, can impact your long-term financial health.

- **Celebrate Milestones**: Recognize and celebrate when you reach a financial milestone, like paying off a credit card or saving a set amount for a down payment. This can provide motivation to stick with your budgeting plan.

Key Takeaways

Maintaining a budget with AI involves regular interaction and engagement with your financial tools, staying proactive about updates and changes in your financial life, and using AI-driven insights to refine and improve your budgeting practices. By following these tips, you can ensure that your AI-assisted budget remains an effective guide towards achieving financial stability and meeting your financial goals.

PART III
Advanced AI Strategies for Credit Score Enhancement

Building on the foundational knowledge and tools covered in earlier sections, Part III of the book delves into advanced strategies for leveraging AI to enhance your credit score. This section will explore innovative AI applications designed to optimize and improve credit profiles, detailing their mechanics, benefits, and how they can be effectively implemented.

Chapter 6: Repairing Your Credit Score with AI

- **AI-Driven Credit Repair Tools:** Discuss tools that identify errors and inconsistencies on credit reports and automate the dispute process with credit bureaus.

- **Optimizing Credit Utilization:** Explain how AI algorithms can suggest optimal credit utilization rates and timely debt payments to improve credit scores.

- **Personalized Credit Improvement Plans:** Detail how AI assesses individual credit situations and recommends bespoke actions to enhance credit scores over time.

Chapter 7: Building Your Credit with AI

- **Establishing Credit History:** Explore AI tools that help users with thin or no credit files by recommending financial products like secured credit cards or credit-builder loans.

- **Smart Credit Management:** Discuss how AI can schedule payments and manage account balances to avoid damaging credit marks.

- **Long-Term Credit Strategy:** Outline how AI can project future credit score changes based on current financial behaviors and suggest adjustments to ensure continual improvement.

Chapter 8: Monitoring and Protecting Credit with AI

- **Comprehensive Credit Monitoring:** Delve into AI systems that monitor credit files across different bureaus, alerting users to potential identity theft or errors affecting scores.

- **Behavioral Pattern Recognition for Fraud Detection:** Illustrate how AI detects unusual activities based on established spending patterns, providing an early warning system against fraud.

- **AI Legal Advisors**: Introduce AI-driven platforms that provide legal advice on credit issues, helping users understand their rights and how to protect or rehabilitate their credit.

Chapter 9: Integrating AI into Everyday Financial Decisions

- **AI Financial Assistants**: Discuss how AI virtual assistants can help manage daily finances, ensuring that all decisions are aligned with credit improvement goals.

- **Dynamic Financial Modeling**: Explain how AI models can simulate different financial scenarios and their potential impacts on credit scores, helping users make informed decisions about large purchases or loans.

- **Education and Continuous Learning**: Cover AI tools that offer educational resources and personalized coaching to improve financial literacy, which is crucial for maintaining a healthy credit score.

Case Studies and Real-World Applications

- **Success Stories**: Provide real-life examples of individuals who significantly improved their credit scores using AI strategies, detailing the challenges they faced and how they overcame them.

- **Comparative Analysis**: Offer a before-and-after analysis of credit scores and financial health to illustrate the tangible benefits of implementing AI-driven credit enhancement strategies.

Key Takeaways

This section of the book empowers readers with cutting-edge AI strategies for actively enhancing their credit scores. By understanding and utilizing these advanced tools and techniques, individuals can not only repair and build their credit effectively but also integrate AI into their everyday financial decisions for ongoing improvement and vigilance. This proactive approach to credit management, backed by AI, can lead to significant financial opportunities and stability, setting the foundation for a secure financial future.

06
Repairing Your Credit Score with AI

Credit repair is a crucial process for those looking to improve their financial health and access better financial opportunities. This chapter explores how Artificial Intelligence (AI) can be utilized to efficiently and effectively repair credit scores. It will cover AI-driven tools and strategies that can identify errors, optimize credit utilization, and provide personalized advice to enhance your credit profile.

AI-Driven Credit Repair Tools

- **Automated Dispute Filings**: Detail how AI tools can automatically detect inaccuracies or outdated information on credit reports, such as wrong account details or duplicate entries, and assist users in filing disputes with credit bureaus directly through the platform.

- **Error Detection Algorithms**: Explain the technology behind AI systems that scan and analyze credit reports to identify potential errors or inconsistencies that may negatively impact a user's credit score.

Optimizing Credit Utilization with AI

- **Utilization Rate Recommendations:** Discuss how AI analyzes current balances and credit limits across all accounts to recommend optimal utilization rates that are likely to improve credit scores.

- **Balancing Transfers and Payments:** Showcase AI strategies that suggest when and how to make balance transfers or adjust payments to manage credit utilization more effectively across multiple accounts.

Personalized Credit Improvement Plans

- **Tailored Recommendations:** Outline how AI tools use personal financial data and credit history to create customized plans for credit improvement, focusing on the most impactful factors for the individual's specific situation.

- **Dynamic Plan Adjustment:** Describe how these plans are not static; AI continuously adjusts recommendations based on new financial data and changes in the credit market, ensuring that users are always working with the most effective strategies.

Implementing AI Tools for Credit Repair

- **Integration with Financial Apps:** Provide a guide on integrating AI credit repair tools with existing financial apps and accounts to ensure seamless monitoring and management.

- **User Engagement and Action:** Stress the importance of user engagement with AI recommendations, including reviewing AI findings, following through on suggested actions, and regularly updating personal information.

Case Studies and Practical Applications

- **Success Story 1**: An individual who corrected multiple credit report errors using an AI-powered tool, resulting in a significant credit score increase.

- **Success Story 2**: A user who optimized their credit utilization with the help of AI, achieving a better score and subsequently qualifying for a lower interest rate on a mortgage.

Challenges and Ethical Considerations

- **Data Privacy**: Discuss concerns related to sharing sensitive financial information with AI platforms and how reputable tools safeguard user data.

- **Dependence on Technology**: Caution about the risks of over-reliance on AI for financial decisions, emphasizing the importance of maintaining personal oversight and understanding of one's credit repair process.

Key Takeaways

This chapter aims to equip readers with knowledge about the potential of AI in repairing credit scores effectively. Through the use of AI-driven tools and strategies, users can identify and correct issues that negatively impact their scores, optimize their credit utilization, and follow personalized plans to improve their credit standings. Engaging with AI in this proactive and informed manner can lead to substantial improvements in financial health and open up new avenues for economic opportunities.

6.1 Identifying Report Errors with AI

Errors in credit reports can have a significant negative impact on your credit score, often through no fault of your own. Artificial Intelligence (AI) can play a crucial role in identifying and rectifying these errors more efficiently than traditional methods. This section explores how AI tools can detect inaccuracies in credit reports, the technology behind these systems, and the steps involved in resolving errors to improve credit scores.

The Importance of Accurate Credit Reports

- **Impact on Credit Scores:** Discuss how errors such as incorrect personal information, outdated account statuses, or wrongful entries can lead to unjustly lowered credit scores.

- **Consequences for Financial Opportunities:** Outline the broader impact of these errors, including higher interest rates on loans, denied loan applications, and potential issues with employment background checks.

How AI Detects Credit Report Errors

- **Data Cross-Verification:** Explain how AI systems cross-verify information across various data points in a credit report against other databases to identify discrepancies. This could involve checking account status reports from different financial institutions or validating personal information against public records.

- **Pattern Recognition:** Detail how machine learning models identify patterns in reporting that typically lead to errors, such as frequent mistakes made by specific data furnishers or common errors in certain types of accounts.

- **Anomaly Detection:** Describe how AI tools use anomaly detection algorithms to flag entries that deviate from normal activity or historical data trends, which could indicate reporting errors.

Steps to Resolve Errors with AI Assistance

- **Automated Dispute Processes:** Show how AI can automate the dispute process by generating and sending dispute letters to credit bureaus with the necessary supporting documentation.

- **Continuous Monitoring:** Discuss how AI tools continue to monitor the user's credit report after disputes are filed to ensure that errors are corrected and to check for the reappearance of previously resolved issues.

- **User Interaction and Confirmation:** Emphasize the importance of user involvement in reviewing AI-detected errors and approving any actions before disputes are filed. This ensures that the dispute process aligns with the user's knowledge of their personal financial records.

Real-World Application

- **Case Study Example:** Provide a case study of an individual who used an AI-powered credit monitoring tool to detect and resolve multiple errors, leading to a substantial improvement in their credit score. Highlight the specific features of the AI tool that contributed to successful error resolution.

Challenges and Limitations

- **Accuracy of AI Predictions:** While AI significantly enhances the error identification process, discuss potential limitations in its ability to discern legitimate discrepancies from legitimate variations in data.

- **Legal and Regulatory Compliance:** Outline the importance of AI tools operating within the bounds of credit reporting laws and regulations, such as the Fair Credit Reporting Act (FCRA), ensuring that users' rights are protected during the dispute process.

Key Takeaways

AI offers a powerful solution for identifying and correcting errors in credit reports, leveraging advanced algorithms to enhance the accuracy and efficiency of these processes. By automating error detection and the dispute process, AI can help individuals more effectively manage their credit health, leading to improved financial opportunities and better overall financial well-being.

6.2 AI Negotiation Tools for Debt Settlement

Negotiating debt settlements can be a daunting task for individuals struggling with debt. Artificial Intelligence (AI) has introduced tools that can assist in this process, making negotiations more accessible and potentially more favorable for the debtor. This section explores how AI can facilitate debt settlement negotiations, including the technology behind these tools, their practical application, and the benefits they offer.

Understanding AI in Debt Negotiation

- **Purpose of AI Negotiation Tools**: Introduce the role of AI tools in debt settlement, which is to act as intermediaries that can negotiate with creditors on behalf of users to reduce the amount owed or alter payment terms.

- **How AI Tools Work**: AI negotiation tools use algorithms to analyze a user's debt situation, predict outcomes based on vast datasets of creditor behaviors, and determine the best strategies for negotiation.

Key Features of AI Negotiation Tools

- **Automated Communication**: Describe how AI systems can automatically communicate with creditors through emails, letters, or even voice calls, presenting proposals for debt settlement that align with what the algorithms determine to be most likely accepted.

- **Customized Negotiation Strategies**: Discuss how these tools personalize negotiation tactics based on the specific debts and creditors involved, as well as the financial profile and goals of the user.

- **Real-Time Adjustments**: Highlight the capability of AI tools to adjust negotiation strategies in real-time based on responses from creditors, optimizing for the best possible outcome.

Practical Steps in AI-Assisted Debt Settlement

- **Initial Debt Analysis**: Users input their debt information into the AI tool, which assesses the total debt, interest rates, and creditor details.

- **Strategy Formulation:** The AI proposes a plan based on the likelihood of creditor acceptance, taking into account historical data and success rates.

- **Engagement and Negotiation:** The AI tool engages with creditors, presenting tailored settlement offers, and managing the negotiation process.

- **Agreement and Closure:** Once a settlement is reached, the AI tool facilitates the agreement process, ensuring all legal and financial documentation is completed accurately.

Benefits of Using AI for Debt Settlement

- **Efficiency:** AI can manage multiple creditor negotiations simultaneously, saving time and increasing the chances of favorable outcomes.

- **Reduced Emotional Stress:** By automating negotiations, AI removes the emotional burden often associated with personal debt settlement discussions.

- **Optimized Settlements:** AI's data-driven approach can lead to more favorable settlement terms than individuals might achieve on their own, potentially reducing debts significantly.

Case Studies and Real-World Applications

- **Success Story:** Provide an example of a user who successfully reduced their overall debt by 40% using an AI negotiation tool, detailing the negotiation process and the strategies used.

- **Comparative Analysis:** Show a side-by-side comparison of outcomes achieved with and without AI assistance, highlighting the effectiveness and impact of AI tools in real-life scenarios.

Challenges and Ethical Considerations

- **Accuracy and Reliability**: Discuss potential concerns about the accuracy of AI decisions and the implications of relying on automated systems for critical financial negotiations.

- **Privacy and Security**: Address how these tools handle sensitive financial data and ensure compliance with financial privacy regulations.

Key Takeaways

AI negotiation tools represent a significant advancement in debt management, providing users with sophisticated, automated, and personalized negotiation services that can lead to substantial debt reductions. By leveraging these tools, individuals can navigate the complex process of debt settlement more effectively, potentially easing financial burdens and accelerating the path to financial recovery.

6.3 Strategies for Long-Term Credit Health

Maintaining and improving your credit health over the long term requires a proactive and informed approach. This section discusses how AI can be leveraged to devise and implement strategies that not only improve credit scores in the short term but also sustain and enhance credit health over time. It will cover the use of AI for ongoing credit management, preventive strategies to avoid credit pitfalls, and tips for using AI tools effectively.

Understanding Long-Term Credit Health

- **Importance of Sustained Credit Health**: Explain why maintaining a good credit score is crucial for financial stability, lower interest rates, and better terms on loans and credit lines over the long term.

- **Components of Long-Term Credit Health**: Discuss the key factors that contribute to sustained credit health, including payment history, credit utilization, length of credit history, and the mix of credit types.

AI-Driven Strategies for Credit Maintenance

- **Continuous Monitoring and Updates**: Highlight how AI tools continuously monitor credit reports and alert users to any changes or potential issues that could impact their credit scores, such as fraudulent activities or reporting errors.

- **Predictive Analytics for Financial Planning**: Discuss how AI uses predictive analytics to forecast future financial scenarios based on current trends and advises on actions that can prevent credit score declines, such as adjusting spending or managing account balances.

- **Automated Credit Utilization Management**: Explain how AI can help maintain optimal credit utilization ratios by suggesting when to pay down balances or when it might be beneficial to increase credit limits.

Preventive Measures and Credit Building

- **Educational Tools and Resources**: Detail how AI platforms offer educational resources that teach users about credit management, including how different financial decisions impact credit scores.

- **Behavioral Coaching**: Introduce AI tools that provide behavioral coaching by analyzing spending habits and offering tailored advice to encourage practices that improve credit health.

- **Debt Management**: Showcase AI strategies for managing and prioritizing debt repayments to avoid high-interest costs and potential hits to credit scores.

Implementing AI Strategies for Long-Term Success

- **Setting Up Automated Systems**: Guide on setting up automated payment systems through AI tools to ensure all bills are paid on time, which is crucial for maintaining a positive payment history.

- **Regular Financial Reviews**: Encourage regular reviews of financial plans using AI tools to adjust goals and strategies as life changes occur, such as a new job, marriage, or buying a house.

- **Integration with Other Financial Tools**: Discuss how integrating AI credit tools with broader financial management systems can provide a holistic view of financial health, allowing for better-informed decisions.

Challenges and Considerations

- **Dependence on Technology**: Caution against over-reliance on AI tools and emphasize the importance of personal involvement and understanding of one's financial health.

- **Data Security and Privacy:** Address potential concerns about the security and privacy of personal and financial data when using AI tools.

Key Takeaways

AI offers powerful strategies and tools for maintaining long-term credit health, providing proactive management and personalized advice that can adapt to changes in financial circumstances. By leveraging these AI-driven strategies, individuals can ensure their credit health remains robust, supporting their overall financial well-being and future goals. This proactive approach, supplemented by regular engagement and education, can pave the way for sustained financial success and stability.

07
Building Your Credit with AI

For many individuals, building a strong credit history is crucial for achieving financial stability. This chapter delves into how Artificial Intelligence (AI) can be utilized to effectively build and enhance credit scores. It will cover various AI-driven tools and strategies that assist in establishing credit, maintaining good credit habits, and ensuring long-term credit health.

Establishing Credit with AI

- **Credit Builder Loans and Accounts**: Introduce AI-driven platforms that recommend specific financial products like secured credit cards or credit builder loans tailored to users' profiles, which can help establish or rebuild credit.

- **Automated Account Management**: Discuss how AI tools can manage these accounts, ensuring that payments are timely and usage rates are optimal to benefit the user's credit score.

AI for Smart Credit Management

- **Payment Optimization**: Explain how AI predicts the best times and amounts to pay on credit accounts to optimize credit score benefits, such as prior to report dates to credit bureaus.

- **Utilization Rate Recommendations**: Detail how AI calculates and suggests ideal credit utilization rates across various accounts to maintain a healthy balance that positively impacts the credit score.

Long-Term Credit Strategy with AI

- **Dynamic Credit Score Improvement Plans:** Outline AI systems that create dynamic, personalized credit improvement plans based on ongoing credit score analysis and financial behavior tracking.

- **Predictive Credit Modeling:** Highlight how AI uses historical data and predictive modeling to forecast future credit score changes and provides recommendations to mitigate risks and improve credit scores over time.

Integrating AI into Everyday Financial Decisions

- **AI Financial Assistants:** Discuss how AI virtual assistants integrate into daily financial decisions, advising on credit-related decisions like spending limits, large purchases, or when to apply for new credit.

- **Real-Time Alerts and Notifications:** Explain how AI tools offer real-time alerts for key activities that affect credit building, such as reaching credit limits or potential opportunities for improving credit mix.

Case Studies and Real-World Applications

- **Success Story 1:** Share a story of an individual who used an AI tool to strategically build their credit from the ground up after bankruptcy, outlining specific AI recommendations followed and the outcomes achieved.

- **Success Story 2**: Describe how a small business owner utilized AI to manage business credit lines, improving both personal and business credit scores through strategic AI-guided actions.

Challenges and Considerations

- **Reliance on Algorithms**: Caution about the risks of relying solely on AI recommendations without understanding the underlying credit principles.

- **Data Privacy and Security**: Emphasize the importance of ensuring that AI tools comply with data protection regulations to safeguard personal information.

Key Takeaways

This chapter illustrates that AI can be a powerful ally in building and maintaining credit health. By leveraging AI-driven tools and strategies, users can not only establish credit more effectively but also enhance their credit scores through informed and timely decisions. The integration of AI into credit management empowers individuals to take control of their financial destinies with confidence and precision.

7.1 Establishing Credit with AI Assistance

Establishing a robust credit history is essential for anyone starting their financial journey or looking to rebuild after financial setbacks. This section delves into how Artificial Intelligence (AI) can assist individuals in establishing credit effectively, outlining the tools and strategies that leverage AI to facilitate this critical process.

The Role of AI in Establishing Credit

- **Introduction**: Explain the importance of establishing credit and how AI can simplify and enhance this process for individuals with limited or no credit history.

- **Targeted Product Recommendations**: Discuss how AI analyzes financial behavior and personal data to recommend the most appropriate financial products for building credit, such as secured credit cards, credit builder loans, or small personal loans.

AI-Driven Strategies for Credit Building

- **Secured Credit Cards**: Detail how AI tools can suggest secured credit card offers based on the user's financial situation, ensuring that the card features align with the user's capability to make regular payments.

- **Credit Builder Loans**: Explain how AI evaluates which credit builder loans are best suited to a user's specific financial conditions and how these loans function to gradually build a user's credit score by ensuring the loan payments are reported to credit bureaus.

- **Automated Payment Features**: Highlight AI functionalities that automate payment schedules to ensure timely payments, thereby building a positive payment history which is crucial for a good credit score.

Optimizing Initial Credit Experiences

- **Smart Credit Utilization**: AI algorithms can guide users on optimal credit utilization, often recommending keeping the balance below 30% of the credit limit, which is crucial in the early stages of building credit.

- **Dynamic Adjustment of Credit Activities**: Discuss how AI can dynamically suggest adjustments in credit activities based on real-time financial behavior and external economic conditions.

Integration with Financial Education

- **Educational Resources**: Introduce AI-driven educational platforms that provide users with knowledge about credit scores, the importance of credit history, and how to manage credit wisely.

- **Behavioral Coaching**: Explain how AI platforms can serve as financial coaches, offering tips and reminders about credit use, such as warnings against high-risk credit behaviors.

Practical Applications and Case Studies

- **Case Study 1**: Showcase a scenario where an individual successfully established a solid credit score from scratch using AI recommendations for secured credit products and automated payment setups.

- **Case Study 2**: Provide an example of someone who improved their initially poor credit score by following AI-driven advice tailored to their changing financial situation.

Challenges and Limitations

- **Dependence on Accurate Data**: Stress the importance of providing accurate financial information to AI systems to ensure the recommendations are suitable and effective.

- **Privacy Concerns**: Address potential privacy issues concerning the sharing of personal and financial data with AI systems and how reputable AI services mitigate these risks.

Key Takeaways

AI provides invaluable assistance in establishing credit by offering tailored financial product recommendations, automating payments, and providing ongoing credit education and management advice. For those new to credit or looking to rebuild, AI can simplify the process, help avoid common pitfalls, and set a foundation for good credit habits that sustain long-term financial health. This proactive and informed approach can help individuals navigate the complexities of credit and leverage opportunities to build a solid financial future.

7.2 AI Tools for Building a Credit History

Building a solid credit history is pivotal for financial stability and access to credit options. This section explores various AI tools that aid in building credit history, detailing their functionalities, benefits, and how they can be strategically used to establish and maintain a strong credit score.

Overview of AI Tools for Credit Building

- **Purpose and Importance**: Introduce how AI tools can assist users in building a credit history, particularly beneficial for those with little to no credit or looking to rebuild after financial setbacks.

- **Types of Tools**: Highlight different AI tools, including financial apps that integrate credit building features, AI-driven financial advisors, and specialized credit building services.

Key AI Tools and Their Functions

- **Credit Simulation Tools**: Discuss tools that simulate various credit scenarios and their impact on a user's credit score. These simulators can guide users on the potential benefits of certain financial actions, such as paying off a particular balance or opening a new account.

- **Automated Credit Reporting**: Some AI tools facilitate reporting rent and utility payments to credit bureaus, traditionally not reported but crucial for building a credit history when managed correctly.

- **Secured Credit Card Managers**: AI can manage secured credit card accounts by optimizing deposit amounts, managing expenditures, and ensuring that utilization stays within the ideal range to build credit effectively.

Enhancing Credit Through AI-Driven Strategies

- **Payment Optimization**: AI algorithms can schedule payments in a way that maximizes positive reporting to credit bureaus, ensuring all payments are made on time and even slightly ahead of schedule to bolster credit scores.

- **Credit Utilization Advice**: Provide guidance on maintaining optimal credit utilization ratios, offering real-time adjustments based on current balances and upcoming expenditures.

- **Long-term Planning**: AI tools can project future credit score trajectories based on current financial habits, helping users understand and plan for long-term credit health.

Practical Applications and User Experiences

- **Integration with Banking Apps**: Many banking apps now incorporate AI-driven credit tools that help users manage their accounts with credit building in mind. Highlight how these integrations make credit management part of everyday banking.

- **Success Stories**: Share real-world examples where users have significantly improved their credit scores using these AI tools, emphasizing the specific features that were most beneficial.

Challenges and Ethical Considerations

- **Data Accuracy and Privacy**: Address concerns about the accuracy of the data used by AI tools and the privacy implications of sharing financial information.

- **Dependence on Technology**: Discuss the potential risks associated with over-reliance on AI for financial decisions, emphasizing the importance of personal oversight and understanding.

Key Takeaways

AI tools offer powerful support in building credit history by providing personalized advice, automating financial decisions, and simulating credit score outcomes. These tools can help users navigate the complexities of credit systems, making strategic decisions that enhance their financial stability. By leveraging AI, individuals can achieve a better understanding of how credit works and how best to engage with financial products to build a strong credit history. This proactive approach can lead to improved access to better financial opportunities and a more secure financial future.

7.3 Preventing Credit Score Decline

Maintaining a healthy credit score is essential for financial flexibility and access to the best credit terms. However, various factors can lead to a decline in credit score. This section explores how AI tools can be leveraged to prevent such declines by monitoring financial activities and providing proactive recommendations.

Understanding Credit Score Dynamics

- **Key Factors Affecting Credit Scores:** Recap the major factors that impact credit scores, including payment history, credit utilization, the length of credit history, types of credit used, and recent credit inquiries.

- **Common Pitfalls:** Discuss common behaviors that lead to credit score declines, such as late payments, high credit card balances, and frequent credit applications.

AI Strategies for Maintaining Credit Scores

- **Real-Time Monitoring and Alerts:** Explain how AI tools offer continuous monitoring of credit activities, alerting users to actions that might negatively impact their credit scores, such as a high utilization rate or a missed payment.

- **Predictive Analysis for Financial Management:** Detail how AI uses predictive analytics to forecast future financial scenarios based on current spending patterns. This can help users make informed decisions to avoid behaviors that may lead to credit score declines.

- **Automated Payment Systems:** Highlight AI systems that can automate payments for loans and credit cards, ensuring payments are always on time, which is crucial for maintaining a good credit score.

Proactive Credit Management with AI

- **Customized Financial Advice:** Discuss how AI tools analyze individual financial situations and provide tailored advice on how to manage credit effectively. This might include suggestions on when to pay off certain debts or when it might be beneficial to request a credit limit increase.

- **Budget Adjustments:** Explain how AI can help adjust budgets in real-time, ensuring that users do not overspend and that enough funds are always available for debt payments, which is essential for credit score health.

- **Debt Repayment Planning:** Explore how AI assists in planning and prioritizing debt repayments in a manner that positively impacts credit scores, such as advising on debt avalanche or snowball methods based on the user's specific credit and financial situation.

Integrating AI Tools for Holistic Credit Management

- **Comprehensive Financial Platforms**: Describe how integrating AI tools with broader financial management platforms provides a holistic view of a user's financial health, helping to manage not just credit but overall financial stability.

- **Long-Term Credit Health Monitoring**: Discuss the benefits of long-term credit health strategies that AI can help develop, including adjusting financial habits and planning for future credit use to ensure continued good credit standing.

Case Studies and Practical Insights

- **Real-World Examples**: Share stories of individuals who successfully used AI tools to prevent potential declines in their credit scores and improve their financial health.

- **Lessons Learned**: Provide insights into the lessons learned from these case studies, emphasizing effective strategies and common pitfalls to avoid.

Key Takeaways

AI offers powerful tools and strategies for preventing declines in credit scores by providing real-time monitoring, predictive analytics, and personalized financial management advice. By utilizing these AI capabilities, users can not only safeguard their credit scores but also enhance their overall financial health, ensuring they remain on a path to financial stability and success.

PART IV
Real-World Applications and Future Trends

This section of the book transitions from theoretical concepts and strategies to real-world applications of AI in credit management, while also exploring emerging trends that could shape the future of personal finance. Through practical examples, case studies, and an examination of evolving technologies, this part aims to provide readers with a comprehensive understanding of how AI tools are currently used and what the future may hold for AI in the credit industry.

Chapter 8: Case Studies of AI in Credit Improvement

- **Success Stories:** Present detailed case studies of individuals and businesses that have successfully utilized AI tools to improve their credit scores. These stories will illustrate specific AI strategies and tools in action, highlighting the practical benefits and challenges encountered.

- **Business Applications:** Explore how companies integrate AI in managing corporate credit, enhancing customer credit offerings, and automating financial services. Include examples from fintech startups and traditional financial institutions.

Chapter 9: AI Credit Assistance in Action

- **Consumer Credit Management:** Discuss various consumer-focused AI applications currently on the market, such as AI-driven personal finance assistants, credit monitoring services, and debt negotiation tools. Highlight the features, user experiences, and effectiveness of these tools.

- **Innovative Credit Models:** Examine how AI is being used to develop more inclusive and comprehensive credit scoring models that consider alternative data, potentially opening up credit to underserved populations.

Chapter 10: The Future of AI and Credit Management

- **Predictive Technologies:** Dive into how AI is expected to enhance its predictive capabilities in personal finance, offering not just reactive tools but proactive financial planning and advisory services.

- **Integration with Blockchain and Other Technologies:** Speculate on the potential integration of AI with blockchain for improved security and transparency in credit transactions and record-keeping.

- **Ethical and Regulatory Considerations**: Discuss the ethical implications of AI in finance, including privacy concerns and the need for regulation to ensure fairness and accountability in AI-driven credit decisions.

Emerging Trends and Innovations

- **Personalized Financial Products**: Look at how AI is leading to the creation of highly personalized financial products that adapt to individual credit behaviors and needs.

- **Global Impact**: Consider the global implications of AI in credit management, especially in developing countries where access to credit is limited. Discuss how AI can transform financial inclusion on a global scale.

- **Advanced Analytics and Machine Learning**: Analyze advancements in machine learning algorithms and data analytics that promise to further refine credit scoring models and financial advisory services.

Key Takeaways

Part IV aims to bridge the gap between theoretical knowledge and practical application, providing readers with a vivid picture of how AI is currently transforming credit management and what future advancements might entail. By understanding these applications and trends, readers can better anticipate changes in the financial landscape and make informed decisions about leveraging AI in their personal and professional lives. This section not only highlights the current state of AI in the credit industry but also inspires optimism and caution about its evolving role in shaping financial services.

08
Case Studies of AI in Credit Improvement

In this chapter, we delve into real-life examples of how Artificial Intelligence (AI) has been successfully utilized to improve credit scores and manage financial health. By examining specific case studies, we gain insights into the practical applications, effectiveness, and transformative potential of AI in credit management.

Case Study 1: Individual Credit Repair

- **Background:** Sarah, a marketing consultant, struggled with a low credit score due to past missed payments and high credit card balances.

- **AI Intervention:** Sarah used an AI-driven credit monitoring tool that identified inaccuracies and outdated information on her credit report. The tool automatically initiated disputes with credit bureaus.

- **Outcome:** Within six months, errors were corrected, and her credit score increased by over 50 points. The AI tool also advised on debt repayment strategies, further enhancing her score.

- **Lessons Learned:** This case highlights the importance of accuracy in credit reports and the effectiveness of AI in automating the dispute resolution process.

Case Study 2: Small Business Credit Optimization

- **Background**: A small online retailer needed to improve its credit score to qualify for a business expansion loan.

- **AI Intervention**: The business employed an AI financial advisor to optimize its credit utilization and payment timings. The AI analyzed cash flow patterns to recommend ideal times for debt payments to maximize credit score benefits.

- **Outcome**: The retailer saw an improvement in their credit score within four months, enabling them to secure a loan with favorable terms.

- **Lessons Learned**: AI's capability to analyze and act on complex data can be crucial for businesses looking to improve financial health quickly and efficiently.

Case Study 3: Overcoming Financial Hardship

- **Background**: Tom, a freelance graphic designer, experienced a drastic drop in income due to a health issue, leading to high credit utilization and a declining credit score.

- **AI Intervention**: Tom used an AI-powered budgeting and credit management tool that adjusted his spending limits, managed bill payments, and prioritized his financial obligations to improve his credit standing.

- **Outcome**: The tool helped Tom maintain his credit score during his illness and slowly improve it as his health and income recovered.

- **Lessons Learned**: AI tools can provide critical support in managing finances during unpredictable life events, helping to maintain and slowly improve credit health.

Case Study 4: Real Estate Investment Firm

- **Background**: A real estate firm wanted to optimize its portfolio and improve its credit score to unlock better financing options.

- **AI Intervention**: The firm implemented an AI system that provided insights on credit impact investments and optimized debt ratios across its portfolio.

- **Outcome**: Improved credit ratings allowed the firm to access lower interest rates and better investment opportunities.

- **Lessons Learned**: AI can play a strategic role in financial decision-making at the corporate level, offering scalable solutions for credit improvement.

Key Takeaways

These case studies illustrate the diverse applications of AI in credit improvement across different scenarios, from individual credit repair to corporate financial strategy. They underscore AI's role in providing personalized, data-driven recommendations and actions that lead to tangible improvements in credit scores. By integrating AI into credit management strategies, both individuals and businesses can not only rectify past financial issues but also pave the way for future financial success. This chapter not only serves as an inspiration but also as a practical guide for those looking to leverage AI to enhance their financial standing.

8.1 Detailed Analysis of Successful Cases

This section provides a more granular look at the successful applications of AI in credit improvement, examining the specific methods, tools, and outcomes of several case studies. The detailed analysis aims to uncover the underlying mechanisms of AI's impact on credit scores and provide actionable insights that can be applied by others.

Case Study 1: Comprehensive Credit Report Correction

- **Background**: Emily, an elementary school teacher, discovered several inaccuracies in her credit report, including wrong account statuses and incorrect late payment entries.

- **AI Tool Used**: Emily used a credit repair AI tool that scans credit reports for discrepancies against known financial data and automatically files disputes with credit bureaus.

- **Process and Intervention**:
    - The AI tool identified errors and auto-generated dispute letters, which were sent to three major credit bureaus.
    - It monitored the response from the credit bureaus and updated Emily on the status of her disputes.
    - AI suggested minor credit behavior adjustments to optimize her score during the dispute process.

- **Outcome**: Her credit score increased by 80 points after the corrections were made, significantly improving her eligibility for a home loan.

- **Analysis**: This case highlights the efficacy of AI in automating the time-consuming dispute process and the importance of proactive credit report monitoring.

Case Study 2: AI-Driven Debt Repayment Planning

- **Background**: Mark, a freelance photographer, was struggling with high credit card debt across multiple accounts.
- **AI Tool Used**: An AI debt repayment planner that analyzes debt accounts, interest rates, and cash flow to optimize payment schedules.
- **Process and Intervention**:
  - The tool prioritized debts with the highest interest rates and suggested a payment schedule that aligned with Mark's irregular income.
  - It adjusted recommendations based on real-time income data and expenditure patterns.
  - Mark received monthly updates and recommendations for extra payments whenever his income spiked.
- **Outcome**: Mark was able to clear his high-interest debt 40% faster than expected and improved his credit score by optimizing his credit utilization.
- **Analysis**: This case demonstrates how AI can tailor debt repayment strategies to individual financial situations, helping to manage and eliminate debt efficiently.

Case Study 3: Building Credit History with AI

- **Background:** Aisha, a recent college graduate, had no credit history and found it difficult to obtain her first credit card.

- **AI Tool Used:** A financial AI assistant that recommends credit-building products suited to users with thin or no credit files.

- **Process and Intervention:**
    - AI recommended a secured credit card and a small credit builder loan, explaining the benefits and risks of each.
    - It set reminders for payments and suggested spending limits to keep utilization low.
    - Aisha used the tool to track her progress and adjust her spending habits based on AI feedback.

- **Outcome:** Within a year, Aisha established a credit score in the 'good' range, allowing her to apply for unsecured credit cards and a car loan.

- **Analysis:** Aisha's case underscores the potential of AI to guide young or new credit users in establishing a healthy credit profile from scratch.

Key Takeaways

The detailed analysis of these cases shows that AI not only provides automation but also personalizes financial advice, making it a powerful tool for credit improvement. By harnessing the capabilities of AI, individuals can navigate their credit journeys more effectively, addressing issues from inaccuracies in credit reports to optimizing debt repayment and establishing new credit. These success stories serve as models for leveraging technology to achieve financial goals and enhance credit health.

8.2 Lessons Learned from AI Credit Enhancements

Reflecting on the successful applications of AI in credit improvement detailed in previous sections, this chapter synthesizes key lessons learned and best practices that can be drawn from these case studies. Understanding these insights can empower users to more effectively leverage AI tools in their personal credit management strategies.

Personalization is Key

- **Tailored Solutions**: AI's ability to analyze individual financial data and provide customized recommendations was crucial in all successful case studies. Users benefited significantly from strategies specifically tailored to their unique financial situations.

- **Lesson**: Engage with AI tools that offer personalized insights and adjustments, ensuring that recommendations are directly applicable to your financial habits and goals.

Proactive Monitoring and Response

- **Continuous Oversight**: Continuous monitoring of credit reports and financial behaviors helped users identify and address issues before they could significantly impact credit scores.

- **Lesson**: Utilize AI tools that provide ongoing monitoring and real-time alerts to maintain an accurate and up-to-date understanding of your credit status and financial health.

Integration Across Financial Behaviors

- **Holistic Financial Management**: AI tools that integrated credit improvement strategies with broader financial management—such as budgeting and debt repayment—proved more effective in enhancing credit scores.

- **Lesson**: Look for comprehensive AI solutions that can manage multiple aspects of personal finance, not just credit, to ensure all financial decisions are aligned and mutually supportive.

The Importance of Educative Interactions

- **Learning and Adaptation**: Case studies showed that users who interacted regularly with AI tools and learned from the insights provided saw more substantial and sustained improvements in their credit scores.

- **Lesson**: Actively engage with AI tools to understand the rationale behind recommendations and adapt your financial strategies accordingly. Treat AI interactions as learning opportunities.

Automation Enhances Compliance

- **Timeliness of Payments**: Automated payment features in AI tools helped users maintain perfect payment histories, significantly boosting their credit scores.

- **Lesson**: Use automation to manage recurring financial obligations, such as bill payments or debt repayments, to avoid human errors like forgetfulness or mismanagement.

Ethical and Privacy Considerations

- **Trust and Security**: While AI tools can significantly improve financial management, issues around data security and privacy remain concerns for many users.
- **Lesson**: Ensure that any AI tool used complies with relevant privacy laws and regulations and maintains the highest standards of data security. Be proactive in understanding how your financial data is used and protected.

Future Preparedness

- **Adaptability to Changing Technologies**: As AI and related technologies evolve, new opportunities and challenges in credit management will emerge.
- **Lesson**: Stay informed about developments in AI and finance technology to continuously adapt and optimize your credit management strategies.

Key Takeaways

The lessons learned from AI-enhanced credit improvements underscore the transformative potential of technology in personal finance. By adopting a proactive, informed, and engaged approach to using AI tools, individuals can not only rectify existing credit issues but also establish robust frameworks for ongoing financial health and stability. These insights are essential for anyone looking to harness AI in their journey towards achieving and maintaining excellent credit.

09
The Future of AI in Credit Management

As we look ahead, the role of Artificial Intelligence (AI) in credit management is poised to expand and evolve, offering new and innovative ways to understand, improve, and utilize credit. This chapter explores potential future developments in AI technologies that could significantly impact the credit management landscape, examining both the opportunities and challenges these advancements may present.

Advanced Predictive Analytics

- **Enhanced Forecasting**: Future AI systems will likely offer even more advanced predictive analytics, capable of highly accurate forecasts regarding credit score changes based on specific financial behaviors or market conditions.

- **Personal Financial Planning**: AI could provide individualized, long-term financial planning assistance, suggesting when to take on new credit, how to optimize debt repayment, or when to save, based on predictive outcomes.

Integration with Emerging Technologies

- **Blockchain for Credit Transactions**: Integration of AI with blockchain technology could revolutionize credit reporting and scoring by enhancing the accuracy, transparency, and security of credit transactions.

- **Internet of Things (IoT) and Credit Management**: IoT devices could feed real-time financial data to AI systems, allowing for more dynamic credit management and instant adjustments based on spending behavior detected through smart devices.

AI and Regulatory Technology

- **Compliance Automation**: AI could automate compliance in credit reporting, ensuring that all data adheres to evolving regulations such as the Fair Credit Reporting Act (FCRA) without human intervention.
- **Fraud Detection**: Enhanced AI algorithms could better detect patterns indicative of fraud or identity theft, reducing losses for consumers and lenders alike.

Ethical AI in Credit Scoring

- **Bias Mitigation**: As AI systems become more sophisticated, the focus will intensify on designing algorithms that minimize bias in credit scoring and lending practices, ensuring fairer credit opportunities for all demographic groups.
- **Transparent AI Systems**: Future developments might focus on creating AI systems that can explain their decision-making processes in understandable terms, increasing transparency and trust in AI-driven credit decisions.

Global Impact and Financial Inclusion

- **Expanding Access to Credit:** AI could play a pivotal role in expanding access to credit in underserved markets, using alternative data points to evaluate creditworthiness for individuals without traditional credit histories.

- **Microfinance and AI:** AI could enhance microfinance initiatives by accurately predicting credit risk and loan repayment probabilities, even in less economically developed regions.

Challenges and Considerations

- **Privacy Concerns:** As AI systems become more embedded in financial operations, managing and protecting personal data will become increasingly critical.

- **Dependency Risks:** There's a risk of over-reliance on AI tools for credit decisions, potentially leading to vulnerabilities if these systems fail or are compromised.

- **Regulatory Evolution:** Regulatory frameworks will need to evolve in tandem with technological advancements to address new challenges posed by AI in credit management.

Key Takeaways

The future of AI in credit management is rich with potential but also fraught with challenges. As AI technologies continue to develop, they promise to transform the credit landscape by making credit management more accurate, efficient, and inclusive. However, the successful integration of these technologies will require careful consideration of ethical implications, privacy issues, and regulatory compliance. Embracing these advancements while conscientiously addressing their challenges will be crucial for maximizing the benefits of AI in credit management for all stakeholders involved.

9.1 Emerging Trends in AI and Finance

The intersection of Artificial Intelligence (AI) and finance is rapidly evolving, driven by advancements in technology and increasing demand for more efficient and personalized financial services. This section explores emerging trends in AI that are shaping the future of finance, particularly in credit management, investment strategies, and personal banking.

Enhanced Personalization in Financial Services

- **Hyper-Personalized Banking**: AI is enabling banks and financial institutions to offer highly personalized experiences, from tailored banking advice to customized financial products based on individual spending habits, lifestyle choices, and financial goals.

- **Personalized Risk Assessment**: AI's ability to analyze vast amounts of data allows for more precise risk assessments, leading to more personalized credit scoring systems that consider a broader range of factors than traditional methods.

Automation and Real-Time Decision Making

- **Automated Real-Time Decisions**: Financial institutions are increasingly using AI to make real-time decisions on credit, investments, and risk management, which enhances efficiency and responsiveness to market changes.

- **Robotic Process Automation (RPA)**: RPA in finance is growing, automating routine tasks like data entry and compliance checks, which speeds up processes and reduces errors.

AI-Driven Financial Advisory and Wealth Management

- **Robo-Advisors**: These AI-driven platforms are becoming more sophisticated, offering not just automated investment suggestions but also holistic financial planning services.

- **AI in Portfolio Management**: AI algorithms can manage investment portfolios with a level of precision and adaptability that is challenging for human managers, continuously analyzing market conditions and adjusting investments accordingly.

Advances in Credit Scoring Models

- **Alternative Data in Credit Scoring**: AI is being used to incorporate alternative data (such as rent payments, utility bills, and even social media activity) into credit scoring models, potentially improving access to credit for those with limited traditional credit history.

- **Dynamic Credit Scoring**: Future AI models may update credit scores in real-time, reflecting the current financial behavior of individuals more accurately and swiftly than the periodic updates used today.

Blockchain and AI Integration

- **Enhanced Security and Transparency:** The combination of blockchain technology with AI is set to revolutionize financial security and transparency, especially in credit transactions and identity verification processes.

- **Smart Contracts:** AI can automate and optimize the execution of smart contracts in blockchain networks, further enhancing efficiency and reducing the potential for disputes.

Ethical AI and Regulatory Compliance

- **Ethical AI Frameworks:** As AI takes on more decision-making roles in finance, the development of ethical AI frameworks is critical to ensure decisions are fair and unbiased.

- **Compliance Monitoring:** AI tools are increasingly being deployed to monitor and ensure compliance with evolving financial regulations globally, helping institutions avoid hefty fines and legal challenges.

The Global Reach of AI in Finance

- **Financial Inclusion:** AI is poised to play a crucial role in enhancing financial inclusion by providing low-cost financial services and credit to underserved populations in emerging markets.

- **Cross-Border Financial Services:** AI facilitates more efficient cross-border transactions and financial services, reducing costs and improving access to global markets for businesses and consumers alike.

Key Takeaways

Emerging trends in AI are transforming the finance sector by enabling more personalized services, enhancing decision-making processes, and improving regulatory compliance. As these technologies continue to evolve, they promise to reshape how financial institutions operate, how they interact with customers, and how they manage risks and opportunities. However, navigating this transformation will require careful attention to the ethical implications, privacy concerns, and regulatory challenges associated with AI in finance.

9.2 How to Stay Ahead with AI

In the rapidly evolving landscape of AI and finance, staying informed and adaptable is crucial for both businesses and individuals who wish to leverage these technologies effectively. This section provides strategies and insights on how to stay ahead in the field of AI-driven finance, ensuring readiness for upcoming trends and maintaining a competitive edge.

Continuous Learning and Adaptation

- **Lifelong Learning**: Encourage ongoing education in AI and related technologies. This can be achieved through online courses, webinars, attending conferences, and staying updated with the latest research and case studies in AI finance.

- **Adaptive Strategy Development**: Develop strategies that are flexible and can quickly adapt to incorporate new AI technologies and insights. This involves regular reassessment and fine-tuning of AI tools and methods based on performance and evolving capabilities.

Leveraging Industry Networks and Partnerships

- **Collaboration:** Engage with other professionals and organizations in the AI and finance sectors. Collaborations can lead to shared knowledge, new opportunities, and partnerships that leverage collective strengths in technology and market reach.

- **Industry Consortia:** Join or form consortia that focus on the development and regulation of AI in finance. These groups can help set industry standards and influence policy making, ensuring that members are at the forefront of industry developments.

Investment in AI Capabilities

- **Technological Infrastructure:** Invest in robust technological infrastructure that supports advanced AI applications. This includes secure cloud storage, high-speed computing resources, and access to AI development platforms.

- **Talent Acquisition:** Attract and retain top talent in AI and data science. Investing in skilled personnel ensures that your organization can not only keep up with AI advancements but also drive innovation internally.

Ethical AI Practices

- **Develop Ethical Guidelines:** Establish clear guidelines on the ethical use of AI, focusing on transparency, accountability, and fairness. Ensuring these principles are at the core of your AI initiatives can enhance trust and sustainability.

- **Impact Assessments**: Regularly conduct impact assessments for AI deployments, evaluating potential effects on customers and the business to mitigate risks associated with bias, privacy breaches, or other ethical concerns.

Proactive Regulatory Compliance

- **Stay Updated on Regulations**: Maintain a proactive approach to understanding and complying with national and international regulations that affect AI in finance. This includes data protection laws, credit reporting standards, and upcoming regulations specific to AI.

- **Engage with Regulators**: Participate in discussions and consultation processes with regulators. This can help shape regulatory frameworks that are conducive to innovation while safeguarding consumer interests and systemic stability.

Customer-Centric AI Innovations

- **Focus on Customer Needs**: Develop AI solutions that address specific customer pain points and enhance user experience. This can involve personalized financial advice, enhanced customer service bots, or streamlined loan application processes using AI.

- **Feedback Mechanisms**: Implement effective feedback mechanisms to gather insights from users about their experiences with AI tools. Use this feedback to continuously improve AI offerings.

Key Takeaways

Staying ahead in AI requires a combination of continuous learning, strategic investment, ethical practices, regulatory vigilance, and a focus on innovation that meets customer needs. By embracing these strategies, organizations and individuals can not only adapt to but also anticipate and shape the future of AI in finance. This proactive approach will ensure that they not only keep pace with technological advancements but also leverage them to achieve strategic advantages and superior outcomes.

9.3 Ethical Considerations in AI Usage

As Artificial Intelligence (AI) becomes more integral to financial services, particularly in credit management, ethical considerations must be at the forefront of its deployment and development. This section discusses the key ethical challenges associated with AI in finance and offers guidelines for addressing these concerns responsibly.

Transparency and Explainability

- **Understanding AI Decisions:** AI systems in finance, especially those involved in credit scoring and lending decisions, should be transparent and explainable. Users and regulators need to understand how decisions are made, particularly if an AI decision adversely affects a customer's credit access.

- **Openness:** Financial institutions should be open about their use of AI, including what data is used, how it is processed, and how it influences decision-making processes. This helps build trust and accountability.

Fairness and Bias Mitigation

- **Identifying and Correcting Bias**: AI systems can inadvertently perpetuate or amplify biases present in historical data, leading to unfair treatment of certain groups. Regular audits and updates are necessary to identify and mitigate biases in AI algorithms.

- **Diverse Data Sets**: Ensure that the data sets used to train AI models are diverse and representative of all demographics to prevent biased outcomes. This includes considering variables that might indirectly lead to discrimination.

Data Privacy and Security

- **Safeguarding Personal Information**: Strict measures should be in place to protect the privacy and security of users' data. This includes compliance with data protection regulations such as GDPR and ensuring that data is encrypted, securely stored, and accessed only when necessary.

- **Consent and Control**: Users should have control over their data, including clear options to consent to how their data is used. Transparency about data usage and the ability to opt-out or control data sharing are critical.

Accountability

- **Clear Lines of Responsibility**: There must be clarity regarding who is responsible for AI decisions in financial services. This includes accountability for errors or when AI-driven decisions lead to financial losses or other adverse effects.

- **Remediation Processes:** Establish clear processes for addressing grievances when AI leads to negative outcomes. Customers should have a straightforward path to dispute AI decisions and seek redress.

Sustainable AI Development

- **Long-term Impacts:** Consider the long-term impacts of AI technology on the financial industry, including potential job displacements and changes in the industry structure. Develop strategies to manage these changes responsibly.

- **Sustainable Practices:** Incorporate sustainability into AI development, including the efficient use of resources and minimizing environmental impact.

Inclusive Financial Practices

- **Enhancing Financial Inclusion:** Use AI to enhance financial inclusion by identifying underserved or marginalized populations and developing products that cater to their needs.

- **Avoiding Exclusivity:** Monitor and prevent scenarios where AI might exclude people from financial services based on opaque or unjustifiable criteria.

Key Takeaways

Ethical considerations are not just add-ons but central to the successful and fair deployment of AI in finance. By prioritizing transparency, fairness, privacy, accountability, sustainability, and inclusivity, financial institutions can harness AI's power responsibly. These practices not only comply with legal requirements but also build trust with customers, enhancing the long-term viability and acceptance of AI in financial services.

Conclusion

Throughout this book, we have explored the transformative power of Artificial Intelligence (AI) in credit management, delving into its applications, benefits, and the challenges it presents. AI's role in finance is rapidly expanding, offering unprecedented opportunities for individuals and businesses alike to optimize their financial health and credit standing.

Recap of Key Themes

- **AI's Role in Credit Management**: We've seen how AI can automate and enhance credit monitoring, dispute resolution, debt management, and budgeting. These tools provide users with real-time insights and proactive recommendations that can significantly improve credit scores and overall financial health.

- **Personalization and Efficiency**: AI's ability to tailor financial advice and automate complex processes not only saves time but also leads to more accurate and effective management of finances. This customization extends from individual consumers to large enterprises, reflecting the broad applicability of AI in diverse financial contexts.

- **Ethical and Regulatory Challenges**: The deployment of AI in finance is not without its challenges. Issues of transparency, fairness, data privacy, and regulatory compliance have been recurring themes, highlighting the need for robust ethical frameworks and stringent oversight.

- **Future Prospects:** Looking ahead, AI is set to further revolutionize the financial sector by integrating with other emerging technologies like blockchain and the Internet of Things (IoT). These advancements promise to enhance the security, efficiency, and inclusivity of financial services, although they will also require new strategies for managing the associated risks.

Final Thoughts

As we stand on the brink of what might be considered a golden era for AI in finance, the potential for AI to aid in credit enhancement is immense. However, the successful integration of these technologies requires not only technical expertise but also a steadfast commitment to ethical practices and continuous adaptation to new challenges and opportunities.

For individuals, embracing AI tools for personal finance means engaging with these technologies thoughtfully—understanding their functionality, benefits, and limitations. For businesses and financial institutions, it involves strategically deploying AI to improve service offerings while navigating the complex landscape of regulatory and ethical considerations.

Ultimately, the journey with AI in finance is one of partnership, where technology serves to amplify human potential and creativity, leading to better financial decisions and healthier economic ecosystems. As we move forward, staying informed, proactive, and responsive to changes will be key to harnessing the full potential of AI in transforming financial landscapes around the globe.

Reflecting on the Journey and Looking Forward

As we conclude this exploration of Artificial Intelligence (AI) in credit management, it is worth reflecting on the journey we have undertaken and the road that lies ahead. The integration of AI into finance has opened new avenues for managing personal and business finances, bringing both profound opportunities and significant challenges.

Reflections on the Journey

- **Evolution of AI**: We began with a basic understanding of AI's capabilities and have seen its application expand into comprehensive tools that manage everything from credit scoring to debt negotiation and budgeting. The evolution from simple automation to complex decision-making assistance marks a significant leap forward in financial technology.

- **Impact on Personal Finance**: For individuals, AI has democratized access to sophisticated financial advice, once the preserve of the wealthy or corporately financed. Today, anyone with a smartphone can access powerful tools to improve their credit score, manage debt, and optimize their financial health.

- **Transformation in Businesses**: For businesses, AI has streamlined operations, enhanced risk management, and provided deeper insights into customer behavior. This transformation is not only about efficiency but also about enabling smarter, data-driven decisions that can lead to sustainable growth.

Lessons Learned

- **Importance of Ethical AI:** One of the crucial lessons from deploying AI in finance is the need for ethical considerations. Issues around transparency, bias, and data privacy have underscored the importance of developing AI in a manner that respects user rights and promotes fairness.

- **Adaptability and Resilience:** Another key takeaway is the importance of adaptability. As financial markets and technologies evolve, so too must the systems and strategies we employ. Resilience in this context means being prepared to continuously learn, adapt, and improve.

Looking Forward

- **Anticipating Technological Convergence:** The future will likely see a convergence of AI with other cutting-edge technologies like blockchain, quantum computing, and IoT. This convergence could redefine what is possible in finance, from ultra-secure transactions to even more personalized banking experiences.

- **Global Impact and Financial Inclusion:** As AI technology becomes more accessible, its potential to impact global financial inclusion grows. By lowering barriers to financial services, AI can play a pivotal role in bringing economic opportunities to underserved populations around the world.

- **Continuous Innovation and Regulation:** Looking ahead, continuous innovation accompanied by thoughtful regulation will be essential. Balancing these two will be key to harnessing

AI's potential while mitigating the risks associated with new technologies.

Final Thoughts

The journey with AI in finance is an ongoing one, characterized by rapid advancements and the constant need for vigilance and adaptation. For all its challenges, the promise of AI to transform financial practices for the better is undeniable. As we look to the future, the focus should be on leveraging AI responsibly, ensuring that it serves to enhance, rather than complicate, our financial lives. Embracing AI in finance with an informed, cautious, and optimistic outlook will enable us to navigate this evolving landscape successfully.

Appendices

The appendices section of this book serves as a resource hub, providing additional information, tools, and references that complement the main content. This section is designed to help readers delve deeper into specific topics, access practical tools, and enhance their understanding of AI in credit management. Here is a structured outline of what the appendices might include:

Appendix A: Glossary of Terms

- **Purpose**: To define key terms and jargon used throughout the book, ensuring that all readers, regardless of their prior knowledge of finance or technology, can fully understand the content.

- **Content**: A comprehensive list of terms such as "Artificial Intelligence," "Credit Utilization," "Blockchain," "Predictive Analytics," and others, each accompanied by a clear, concise definition.

Appendix B: FAQ on AI and Credit Management

- **Purpose**: To address common questions and concerns readers might have about using AI for credit management, based on the themes and inquiries presented in the book.

- **Content**: A curated list of frequently asked questions, providing straightforward answers that aim to clarify complex concepts and resolve common misunderstandings.

Appendix C: Resources for Further Exploration

- **Purpose**: To guide readers interested in furthering their understanding of AI and finance, providing them with a pathway to additional information and learning resources.

- **Content**:
    - **Educational Resources**: Links to online courses, webinars, and workshops on AI, finance, and related subjects.
    - **Reading List**: Recommended books, articles, and research papers that offer deeper insights into specific topics covered in the book.
    - **Online Tools and Applications**: A list of online tools, apps, and software that can help readers apply AI technologies to manage their personal finances.

Appendix D: Regulatory Frameworks and Compliance

- **Purpose**: To inform readers about the legal and regulatory environment surrounding the use of AI in financial services, particularly in credit management.

- **Content**:
    - **Overview of Major Regulations**: Descriptions of key regulations such as the Fair Credit Reporting Act (FCRA), General Data Protection Regulation (GDPR), and others that impact the use of AI in finance.
    - **Compliance Checklist**: A checklist for ensuring that AI applications in finance are compliant with existing laws and regulations.

Appendix E: Case Studies and Data Sets

- **Purpose:** To provide additional case studies and examples that were not included in the main text, offering more detailed insights into the application of AI in different financial scenarios.

- **Content:**

    o **Extended Case Studies:** More comprehensive details on the case studies mentioned, as well as additional examples.

    o **Access to Public Data Sets:** Links to publicly available data sets that can be used for experimenting with AI and credit management simulations.

Key Takeaways

The appendices are intended to enrich the reader's experience and provide a robust support structure for those who wish to engage more deeply with the material or apply the concepts discussed to real-world scenarios. By offering definitions, resources, regulatory guidance, and additional case studies, this section ensures that readers are well-equipped to navigate the complexities of AI in credit management.

Glossary of Terms

This glossary provides definitions for key terms used throughout the book related to Artificial Intelligence (AI) and credit management. Understanding these terms is essential for grasping the complex interactions between AI technologies and financial practices.

A

- **Artificial Intelligence (AI):** A branch of computer science dedicated to creating systems capable of performing tasks that would normally require human intelligence, such as visual perception, speech recognition, decision-making, and language translation.

B

- **Blockchain:** A distributed ledger technology that maintains a secure and decentralized record of transactions across multiple computers. Frequently associated with cryptocurrencies, it has applications in various fields, including financial services for ensuring transparency and security.

C

- **Credit Score:** A numerical expression based on a level analysis of a person's credit files, to represent the creditworthiness of an individual. A higher score indicates better credit health.

- **Credit Utilization Rate:** The ratio of your outstanding credit balances to your credit limits. It is an important factor in calculating credit scores, with lower utilization typically seen as favorable.

- **Credit Bureau:** An agency that collects and maintains individual credit information and sells it to creditors so they can decide whether to lend money to potential borrowers.

D

- **Data Mining**: The practice of examining large pre-existing databases in order to generate new information and find patterns, which can be used for predictive modeling in various applications, including finance.

E

- **Encryption**: The process of converting information or data into a secure format to prevent unauthorized access, a critical aspect of data security in financial transactions and personal data.

F

- **Fintech**: A blend of "financial technology," it refers to new tech that seeks to improve and automate the delivery and use of financial services. It includes innovations in financial literacy, education, retail banking, investment, and more.

G

- **General Data Protection Regulation (GDPR)**: A regulation in EU law on data protection and privacy in the European Union and the European Economic Area, which also addresses the transfer of personal data outside these areas.

I

- **Internet of Things (IoT)**: The network of physical objects—"things"—that are embedded with sensors, software, and other technologies for the purpose of connecting and exchanging data with other devices and systems over the internet.

M

- **Machine Learning**: A subset of AI that involves the study of computer algorithms that improve automatically through experience and by the use of data. It is seen as a vital part of gaining insights from large volumes of data.

P

- **Predictive Analytics**: The use of data, statistical algorithms, and machine learning techniques to identify the likelihood of future outcomes based on historical data. In finance, it can predict behaviors like customer churn, loan defaults, or stock market trends.

R

- **Robotic Process Automation (RPA)**: The technology that allows businesses to automate routine tasks across applications and systems by mimicking human interactions and executing business processes like human users.

S

- **Smart Contracts**: Self-executing contracts with the terms of the agreement between buyer and seller being directly written into lines of code. They allow trusted transactions and agreements to be carried out among disparate, anonymous parties without the need for a central authority, legal system, or external enforcement mechanism.

This glossary is not exhaustive but includes some of the most pertinent terms related to the intersection of AI and credit management as discussed in this book. These definitions should assist readers in better understanding the material covered and facilitate deeper engagement with the topics.

FAQs on AI and Credit Management

This section addresses some frequently asked questions about the use of Artificial Intelligence (AI) in credit management, providing clear, concise answers to help readers understand how AI technologies can impact personal finance and credit decisions.

What is AI in credit management?

AI in credit management refers to the use of machine learning algorithms and data analysis techniques to improve the process of managing credit scores, debt, and financial transactions. AI can automate tasks such as credit scoring, risk assessment, and fraud detection, making these processes more efficient and accurate.

How can AI improve my credit score?

AI can improve your credit score by providing personalized recommendations based on your financial behavior and credit history. It can suggest optimal payment timings, advise on credit utilization, and alert you to potential credit report errors that you might need to dispute. AI tools also help maintain your credit health by monitoring your financial activities and providing real-time feedback.

Is AI reliable for managing credit?

AI is becoming increasingly reliable for managing credit due to advancements in machine learning and big data analytics. However, the reliability often depends on the quality of the data input into AI systems and the sophistication of the algorithms used. It's important to use AI tools from reputable providers and continually monitor their effectiveness.

What are the risks of using AI in credit management?

The primary risks of using AI in credit management include data privacy concerns, the potential for algorithmic bias, and over-reliance on automated systems. Ensuring that AI systems are transparent, ethically developed, and regularly audited can help mitigate these risks. Users should also stay informed and engaged with their credit management, even when using AI tools.

Can AI replace human financial advisors?

While AI can automate many aspects of financial advice, it is not likely to completely replace human financial advisors soon. AI is excellent for processing large amounts of data and handling routine transactions, but human advisors provide value in understanding complex personal circumstances, offering customized advice, and handling nuanced financial planning that AI may not fully grasp.

How do I choose the right AI tool for credit management?

Choosing the right AI tool for credit management involves considering several factors:

1. **Accuracy and Reliability**: Look for tools with proven accuracy and reliability in credit management tasks.
2. **Security**: Ensure the tool adheres to stringent data protection regulations to safeguard your financial information.
3. **User Reviews**: Consider user feedback to gauge the tool's effectiveness and customer satisfaction.
4. **Features**: Match the tool's features with your specific credit management needs, such as credit monitoring, report disputes, or debt management.

How does AI detect fraud in credit management?

AI detects fraud by analyzing spending patterns, transaction histories, and behavioral data to identify anomalies that may indicate fraudulent activity. Machine learning models are trained on vast datasets of fraudulent and non-fraudulent transactions to learn these patterns and provide real-time alerts when potential fraud is detected.

Will AI in credit management become more prevalent in the future?

AI in credit management is expected to become more prevalent and sophisticated due to ongoing advancements in technology and growing demand for efficient financial services. As AI tools become smarter and more integrated into financial systems, their role in credit management is likely to expand, offering more advanced solutions for credit optimization, fraud prevention, and financial planning.

These FAQs provide a broad overview of how AI interacts with credit management, addressing common concerns and highlighting the potential benefits and challenges of integrating AI into personal finance strategies.

Resources for Further Exploration

For readers interested in deepening their knowledge about Artificial Intelligence (AI) in credit management and personal finance, this appendix provides a curated list of resources. These resources include educational platforms, books, and online tools that offer valuable insights and practical knowledge.

Educational Resources

- **Coursera** - Offers a variety of courses on AI, data science, and finance from top universities and companies worldwide. Recommended course: "Machine Learning for All".

- **edX** - Provides access to courses designed by experts from universities like MIT and Harvard. Look for "Data Science and Machine Learning Essentials".

- **Khan Academy** - Features comprehensive lessons on economics and finance fundamentals, which are crucial for understanding the financial contexts in which AI operates.

- **Udemy** - Has a broad range of courses targeting specific skills, including Python for finance, AI in FinTech, and more advanced AI applications.

Books

1. **"Artificial Intelligence in Finance: A Python-Based Guide" by Yves Hilpisch** - A practical guide to implementing AI algorithms in financial markets.

2. **"Machine Learning in Finance: From Theory to Practice" by Matthew F. Dixon, Igor Halperin, and Paul Bilokon** - Provides an in-depth exploration of machine learning techniques in quantitative finance.

3. **"Big Data and Machine Learning in Quantitative Investment" by Tony Guida** - Offers insights into how big data and machine learning are changing investment strategies.

Online Tools and Applications

1. **Mint** - A personal finance app that uses AI to help users track spending and manage budgets effectively.

2. **Credit Karma** - Provides AI-driven insights for credit score improvement and personalized financial product recommendations.

3. **Quicken** - An advanced personal finance management tool that offers investment tracking and budgeting guided by AI.

4. **Zest AI** - Offers a platform specifically designed to provide AI solutions for credit underwriting and risk management.

Professional Organizations and Journals

1. **Association for the Advancement of Artificial Intelligence (AAAI)** - A professional organization devoted to promoting research in, and responsible use of, artificial intelligence.

2. **Journal of Financial Data Science** - Publishes the latest research on the application of data science and AI in finance.

Conferences and Workshops

1. **Finovate** - A series of conferences focusing on innovations in financial and banking technology, often featuring the latest uses of AI.

2. **The AI Summit** - Offers a finance-focused track that discusses the impact of AI on finance, featuring speakers from leading global financial institutions.

Key Takeaways

These resources provide a pathway for readers who wish to further explore the concepts discussed in the book, whether through formal education, reading, or practical tool engagement. By utilizing these resources, readers can gain a more nuanced understanding of AI applications in finance, stay updated with the latest trends, and enhance their ability to implement effective AI strategies in credit management and personal finance.

Index

An index is a valuable tool in any book, especially one covering as many complex topics as AI in credit management. Below is a structured outline for an index that organizes the key terms, concepts, and case studies discussed throughout the book. This will help readers quickly locate information and navigate the book efficiently.

A

- AI Definitions: 136
- AI in Finance: 111
- Automated Payment Systems: 91
- Alternative Data in Credit Scoring: 110

B

- Blockchain Technology: 111
- Bias Mitigation in AI: 136

C

- Credit Score Improvement: 83
- Credit Utilization Strategies:
- Case Studies:
    - Individual Credit Repair: 96
    - Business Credit Management: 136

D

- Data Privacy: 72, 84, 116
- Debt Repayment with AI: 137

E

- Ethical AI: 107, 111, 113
- Explainability in AI: 137

F

- Financial Inclusion: 111
- FAQs on AI and Credit Management: 130

G

- Glossary of Terms: 126

I

- IoT (Internet of Things): 107, 128

M

- Machine Learning: 21, 195
- Microfinance and AI: 108

P

- Predictive Analytics: 33, 106, 129
- Privacy Concerns in AI: 137

R

- Regulatory Compliance: 75
- Robotic Process Automation (RPA): 110, 129

S

- Smart Contracts: 111, 129
- Success Stories:
    - Credit Score Recovery: 94
    - Debt Management: 14, 19, 80

T

- Transparency in AI: 138

Key Takeaways

The index provides a comprehensive roadmap to the various topics discussed, making the book a more accessible and useful resource. By referring to the index, readers can efficiently find information relevant to their specific interests or needs, enhancing their understanding and application of the content.

A Note from Ernie Braveboy

Thank you for taking the time to explore "AI and Credit Management." I hope the insights shared within these pages have equipped you with valuable knowledge and practical tools to navigate the complexities of credit improvement with AI.

If this book has helped you, please consider sharing your experience by leaving a review on Amazon. Your feedback is not only immensely valuable to me but also helps others make informed decisions about exploring similar topics.

Thank you once again for your support, and happy reading!

Warm regards,

Ernie Braveboy

Preview of "Credit Repair: How to Repair Your Credit All by Yourself - A Beginner's Guide to Better Credit"

Are you tired of being held back by a poor credit score? Do high interest rates and denied applications sound all too familiar? Take control of your financial future with "Credit Repair: How to Repair Your Credit All by Yourself." This comprehensive guide is your first step towards financial freedom and a healthier credit score.

What You Will Learn:

- **Understanding Your Credit Score**: Discover what makes up your credit score and why it matters in your everyday life.

- **Identifying Credit Report Errors**: Learn the techniques to spot errors in your credit reports and how to effectively dispute them to improve your score.

- **Debt Management Strategies**: Master the art of managing and reducing your debt load with practical, step-by-step advice.

- **Building a Better Credit History**: Find out how to start from scratch and gradually build a positive credit history through responsible practices.

- **Legal Rights and Credit Repair**: Get acquainted with your legal rights as a consumer in the credit system, ensuring you're protected every step of the way.

Features Include:

- **DIY Credit Repair Walkthroughs**: Detailed walkthroughs that guide you through the process of repairing your credit without the need for expensive credit repair services.

- **Checklists and Templates**: Useful tools to help you organize your efforts and make clear, consistent progress.

- **Expert Tips and Insights**: Gain insights from financial experts on avoiding common pitfalls and enhancing your credit management strategies.

"Credit Repair" is more than just a book; it's a roadmap to a brighter financial future. Written in clear, understandable language, this guide is perfect for beginners and provides actionable steps to help you enhance your credit score and take charge of your financial health.

Purchase your copy today on Amazon and start your journey towards better credit: https://a.co/d/iVHY6L3

Your path to better credit begins here!

Connect With Me on Social Media

Join our vibrant community and stay connected on social media! Follow me for the latest updates, engage in live discussions, and take a peek at the behind-the-scenes of my writing process. Your insights are invaluable, and I enjoy interacting with readers and enthusiasts alike. Participate in polls, enjoy exclusive content, and share your experiences. Here's where you can connect with me:

- **TikTok**: Catch quick tips and lively video content by following me at @erniebraveboy.
- **Facebook**: Become part of our interactive community on Facebook at Ernie Braveboy's Facebook Page.
- **Instagram**: Get visual updates and daily inspirations from my work on Instagram @erniebraveboy.

I love to hear from you, so don't hesitate to reach out and engage on these platforms. Your support and feedback drive my passion and help shape my work. Let's connect!

www.ingramcontent.com/pod-product-compliance
Lightning Source LLC
Chambersburg PA
CBHW070247230526
45470CB00002B/501